THE BILLABLE HOUR

THE BILLABLE HOUR

Bill Smarter. Bill More.

SECOND EDITION

Annie Dike

CAROLINA ACADEMIC PRESS
Durham, North Carolina

ISBN: 978-1-5310-2782-7
eISBN: 978-1-5310-2783-4
LCCN: 2023944573

CAROLINA ACADEMIC PRESS
700 Kent Street
Durham, North Carolina 27701
(919) 489-7486
www.cap-press.com
Printed in the United States of America

CONTENTS

Introduction	3
Bill Ethically	9
Bill by Task not Time Segments	13
Bill in Bites not Blocks	23
Bill More Tasks	43
Bill in More Detail	59
Bill by Guidelines	67
Bill Only Billable Tasks	75
Bill More Paralegal Time	81
Bill More by Keeping Less	93
Timekeeping Software	103
Conclusion	107
Appendix A	109
Appendix B	111
Index	115
About the Author	117

THE BILLABLE HOUR

INTRODUCTION

So, why a book on billing? What are you expecting to get out of this? If you have ever struggled with billing, found yourself at the end of a stressful, busy day, or week, with nothing on paper to show for it, you are going to learn to bill smarter, bill more efficiently and, more importantly, bill more, ethically. You are going to reclaim your lost time. You are going to advance yourself professionally and move your cases forward more efficiently. If you want to bill more — and we all do — this book is for you.

I was once you, a law student, law clerk, recent graduate, new associate, young attorney, older attorney, new to the billable hour or not-so-new to it, but struggling with it all the same. And, like many of you, I received no instruction in law school, and very little when I began the practice, on billing. It was a rare day that anyone sat down with me and showed me what to bill, what not to bill, how to keep up with my time, how to properly describe tasks, etc., which is surprising when billing is such an important part of our practice. Billing is how we prove the work we have done. Billing is how we get paid. We spend a lot of time and money trying to sharpen our litigation skills, learn how to take a better deposition, how to select the right jury, and so on. It would seem equally important to spend some time and money sharpening our billing skills. I have spoken to many attorneys, young and old, who lose time and profit, daily, to poor billing practices, and I have taught them how to reclaim their lost time. You can capture all of your billable tasks, contemporaneously. You can bill more, ethically, and I can show you how. Watch and learn.

Here is a sample time sheet:

File	Time	Task
Smith 13789	0.6	Receipt and review of Notice of Hearing; email to Mr. Client enclosing and discussing same; letter to opposing counsel discussing issues to be addressed at hearing
Turner 14825	6.0	Legal research for summary judgment
Pike 13654	0.6	Travel to Orange County for hearing on Defendant's Motion to Compel
	1.1	Attended hearing in Orange County on Defendant's Motion to Compel
	0.6	Return travel from Orange County for hearing on Defendant's Motion to Compel
	8.9	

You may be thinking that looks pretty good, right? But, let's see what the client thinks of that bill:

File	Time	Task
Smith 13789	~~0.6~~ 0.1	Receipt and review of Notice of Hearing~~; email to Mr. Client enclosing and discussing same; letter to opposing counsel discussing issues to be addressed at hearing~~ *block bill*
Turner 14825	~~6.0~~ 3.0	Legal research for summary judgment *generic entry*
Pike 13654	~~0.6~~	~~Travel to Orange County for hearing on Defendant's Motion to Compel~~
	1.1	Attended hearing in Orange County on Defendant's Motion to Compel
	~~0.6~~	~~Return travel from Orange County for hearing on Defendant's Motion to Compel~~ *travel time–not billable*
	~~8.9~~	5.1

Now let's look at a time sheet documenting the same workday but utilizing The Billable Hour techniques:

File	**Time**	**Task**
Smith 13789	0.1	Receipt and review of Notice of Hearing on Plaintiff's Motion for Reconsideration
	0.2	Email to Mr. Client enclosing the Notice of Hearing for Plaintiff's Motion for Reconsideration and discussing same
	0.3	Prepared letter to opposing counsel discussing Motion for Reconsideration and issues to be addressed at hearing for same
Turner 14825	1.8	Reviewed and compiled state court opinions finding contributory negligence valid defense to product liability claims in preparation for drafting summary judgment brief
	2.4	Reviewed and compiled federal court opinions finding preemption of federal manufacturing regulations over state law in preparation for drafting summary judgment brief
	1.8	Reviewed and compiled state court opinions on proper calculation of lost wages in products liability case in preparation for addressing same in summary judgment brief
Pike 13654	0.5	Reviewed Defendant's Motion to Compel and related pleadings and prepared outline for oral argument at hearing on same
	1.1	Attended hearing in Orange County on Defendant's Motion to Compel
	0.4	Meeting with opposing counsel following hearing on Defendant's Motion to Compel discussing pending discovery requests and related matters
	0.3	Telephone conference with Mr. Client reporting on this morning's hearing before Judge Johnston on Defendant's Motion to Compel
	8.9	ACCEPTED

I probably do not need to ask you which time sheet you would prefer. With this guide, I assure you, the latter can and will be yours. If you are not capturing all of your billable tasks, you are losing time. If you are a law clerk, you are diminishing your likelihood for employment. If you are an associate, you are reducing your prospects for partnership. And, if you are a partner, you are not getting paid for all of the work you are performing. No matter what type of law you practice, if you bill by the hour, these tips and techniques will help you learn to bill more efficiently, and spend less time documenting your time and reviewing your bills, leaving you more time to perform more billable tasks and move your cases forward. You can bill more, easily and ethically. You just have to learn to document your time contemporaneously in a manner that meets client criteria. This guide will show you how. You are doing the work. I want to make sure you get paid for it.

BILL ETHICALLY

Go on. Don't be shy. Ask it. Is this ethical? The professional standards attorneys set for themselves are high, intentionally so. It is a difficult and confusing, but highly regarded profession, fraught daily with ethical dilemmas.

This guide will teach you an efficient, effective billing system that will enable you to identify and perform more billable tasks, resulting in more hours billed and to document your time contemporaneously to ensure it is accurate and fulfills your timekeeping obligation to clients.

ABA MODEL RULES OF PROFESSIONAL CONDUCT

A lawyer shall not make an agreement for, charge, or collect an unreasonable fee or an unreasonable amount for expenses.

ABA Model Rule 1.5

If any of the methods and suggestions in this guide do not suit your practice or preferences, then by all means, do not implement them. You are the attorney. You must exercise your own professional judgment. You are the one who must ensure your billing practices are fair, ethical, and reasonable.

> *'[B]illing judgment' is an important component in fee setting. It is no less important here. Hours that are not properly billed to one's client also are not properly billed to one's adversary pursuant to statutory authority.*
>
> *Copeland v. Marshall*,
> 641 F.2d 880, 891 (D.C. Cir. 1980)

So, that is precisely the right question to ask and it is one you should always ask yourself. Is this ethical? The answer to your question, counselor, is—absolutely. If you purchased this guide in hopes of finding a way to pad your time or bill for tasks you did not perform, this is not the book for you.

> **ABA MODEL RULE 8.4(C)**
>
> *It is professional misconduct for a lawyer to . . . engage in conduct involving dishonesty, fraud, deceit or misrepresentation.*

And, if that is your goal, I cannot help you. Rather, my goal is to teach you how to identify more tasks to perform and bill more effectively for them. It is written with a specific eye to the ethics involved in order to teach you to capture all of your tasks and document them in sufficient detail to negate any confusion or question on the client or court's part about your billable time.

> ***The party requesting fees has the burden of submitting billing records to establish that the number of hours it has requested are reasonable.***
>
> *In re Wash. Pub. Power Supply Sys. Sec. Litig.*,
> 19 F.3d 1291, 1305 (9th Cir. 1994).

> ***A vague billing entry lacks sufficient detail to enable a court to determine what work was actually performed and the time it takes to perform such work.***
>
> *Lindy Bros. Builders, Inc. v. Am. Radiator & Standard Sanitary Corp.*, 487 F.2d 161 (3d Cir. 1973)

This guide will also teach you how to delegate your time-keeping, enabling you to spend less time keeping up with your time and more time doing billable tasks, which means more time billed. Helping you bill more, ethically, is the only goal. This book will also enable you to identify and correct poor billing practices that not only reduce your overall billable hours but also may result in ethical violations or rejection of your invoices by the client or court. Some of these practices include:

- Failing to document time contemporaneously
- Describing tasks in generic or vague terms
- Implementing minimal billing increments greater than six minutes
- Block-billing

> *The party seeking an award of fees should submit evidence supporting the hours worked and rates claimed. Where the documentation of hours is inadequate, the district court may reduce the award accordingly.*
>
> ***Hensley v. Eckerhart*, 461 U.S. 424, 434 (1983)**

You may have been unknowingly doing some of these things before, but you will not anymore. You will bill smarter and you will bill more, easily and ethically. Let's begin.

> ***Forfeiture (of attorney's fee) is similarly mandated if an attorney violates ethical standards, his fiduciary duties to his client or his duty as an officer of the court.***
>
> *In re Damon*, 40 B.R. 367 (S.D.N.Y. 1984); *see also*
> *In re Arlan's Dept. Stores, Inc.*, 615 F.2d 925 (2nd Cir. 1979).

BILL BY TASK NOT TIME SEGMENTS

I have often had attorneys new to billing ask me when they should "start" or "stop" the proverbial billing "clock." Their questions typically take on the following form:

> ***"So, let's say I get an email from the court with a pleading attached. I read the pleading and determine I need to send it to the client. I send it to the client via email and the client comes back immediately with a question, which I answer. When do I start and stop the clock on this?"***

While I certainly understand their confusion and want to help, I hesitate for a moment, because I know this is really going to turn their billable world upside-down, but I know it must be done. *There is no clock.*

At least not in the sense that you can click it "on," start a task, finish it, then click it "off" again, like a stopwatch. It is simply impossible. As you likely know or are learning, it is a very rare day, indeed, in your practice that you have the luxury to spend six, uninterrupted minutes doing one task. It is just not going to happen. Rather, a lawyer's day is a constant barrage of interruptions: client calls, emails, staff questions, meetings, project work which is always interrupted by client calls, emails, staff questions, etc., and the cycle continues. It's called multi-tasking, and it is necessary. Do not try to avoid it by waving a stopwatch at your paralegal and shooing them away until your current "six minutes" has run. If you try to keep up with your time via an imaginary clock that you "click on" and "click off" as you start and finish tasks, you are only going to end up selling yourself short and irritating your staff with the annoying stopwatch bit.

Give it up. There is no clock.

And, I speak from experience, trust me. I tried many times to do it the hard way, before I learned to do it the easy way. The first time sheet that was handed to me in the practice looked something like this — a thick pad of blank time sheets with 8:00 a.m. to 1:00 p.m. on the front and 1:00 p.m. to 5:00 p.m. on the back:

BILL BY TASK NOT TIME SEGMENTS

NAME: ____________ DAY: ____________ DATE: ____________

TIME:	CLIENT/CASE	FILE NO.	SERVICES PERFORMED
8:00			
:12			
:24			
:36			
:48			
9:00			
:12			
:24			
:36			
:48			
10:00			
:12			
:24			
:36			
:48			
11:00			
:12			
:24			
:36			
:48			
12:00			
:12			
:24			
:36			
:48			
1:00			

By noon, that time sheet looked like this. And, by 5:00 p.m., I had cursed it, crumpled it, and thrown it in the trash can.

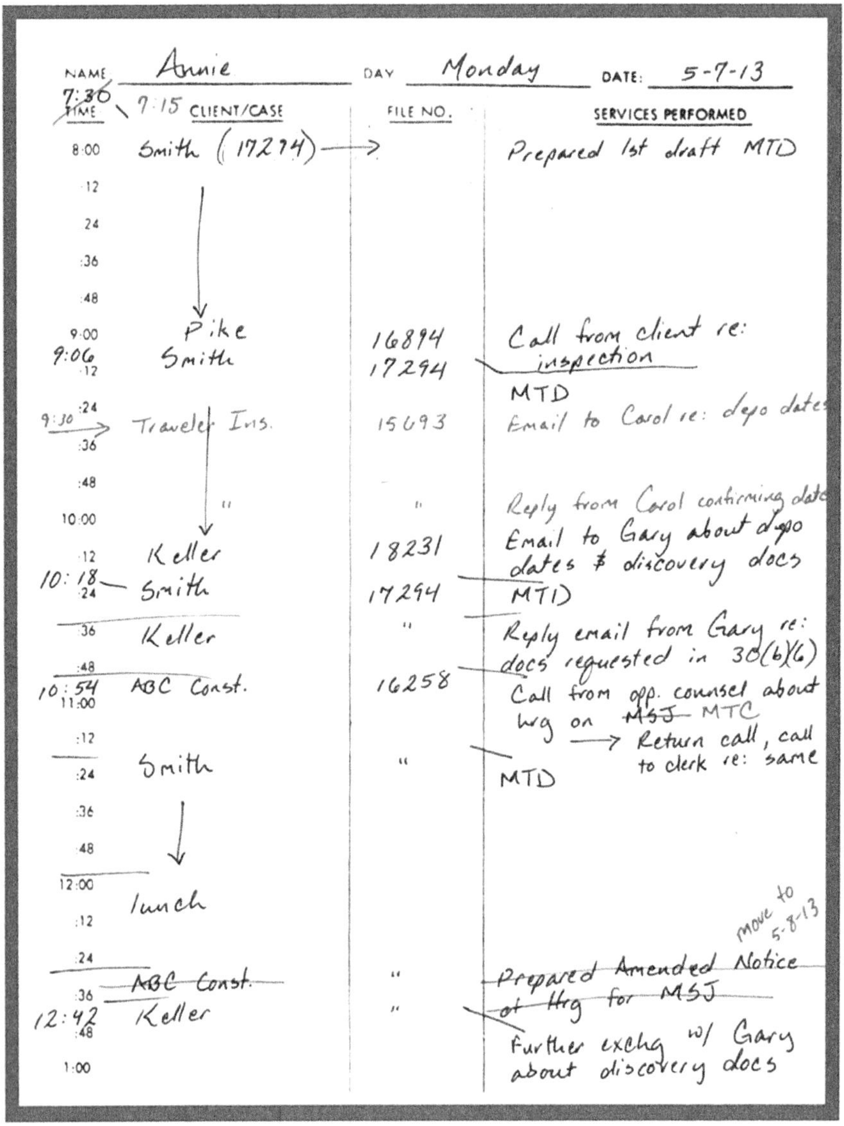

NAME Annie DAY Monday DATE: 5-7-13

TIME ~~7:30~~ 7:15	CLIENT/CASE	FILE NO.	SERVICES PERFORMED
8:00	Smith (17294) →		Prepared 1st draft MTD
:12	↓		
:24			
:36			
:48			
9:00	Pike	16894	Call from client re: inspection
9:06 :12	Smith	17294	MTD
:24 9:30 →	Traveler Ins.	15693	Email to Carol re: depo dates
:36	↓		
:48			
10:00	"	"	Reply from Carol confirming date
:12	Keller	18231	Email to Gary about depo dates & discovery docs
10:18 :24	Smith	17294	MTD
:36	Keller	"	Reply email from Gary re: docs requested in 30(b)(6)
:48			
10:54 11:00	ABC Const.	16258	Call from opp. counsel about hrg on ~~MSJ~~ MTC → Return call, call to clerk re: same
:12			
:24	Smith	"	MTD
:36	↓		
:48			
12:00	lunch		
:12			
:24			move to 5-8-13
:36	~~ABC Const.~~	"	~~Prepared Amended Notice of Hrg for MSJ~~
12:42 :48	Keller	"	Further exchg w/ Gary about discovery docs
1:00			

Finding this time sheet unworkable because it lumped two six-minute time increments together for every entry and because it had to be handwritten, I created my own electronic time sheet that allowed me to type my time entries, but I still tried to enter my tasks according to the specific six-minute segment in the day in which they were performed.

Day: ______________ Date: ______________

	Number	Name	Task	
7:00				
7:06				
7:12				
7:18				
7:24				
7:30				
7:36				
7:42				
7:48				
7:54				
8:00				
8:06				
8:12				
8:18				
8:24				
8:30				
8:36				
8:42				
8:48				
8:54				
9:00				
9:06				
9:12				
9:18				
9:24				
9:30				
9:36				
9:42				
9:48				
9:54				
10:00				
10:06				
10:12				
10:18				
10:24				
10:30				
10:36				
10:42				
10:48				
10:54				
11:00				
11:06				
11:12				
11:18				
11:24				
11:30				
11:36				
11:42				
11:48				
11:54				
12:00				
12:06				
12:12				
12:18				
12:24				
12:30				
12:36				
12:42				
12:48				
12:54				
1:00				
1:06				
1:12				
1:18				
1:24				
1:30				
1:36				
1:42				
1:48				
1:54				
2:00				
2:06				
2:12				
2:18				
2:24				
2:30				
2:36				
2:42				
2:48				
2:54				
3:00				
3:06				
3:12				
3:18				
3:24				
3:30				
3:36				
3:42				
3:48				
3:54				
4:00				
4:06				
4:12				
4:18				
4:24				
4:30				
4:36				
4:42				
4:48				
4:54				
5:00				
5:06				
5:12				
5:18				
5:24				
5:30				
5:36				
5:42				
5:48				
5:54				
6:00				

Overlooking entirely the amount of non-billable time I spent preparing this masterpiece, the real travesty occurred when I actually tried to start using this heinous worksheet. Let's run through a hypothetical, and you will quickly see how cumbersome and unworkable the "clock" time sheet, i.e., billing by time segments, can be.

At the bright morning hour of 8:00 a.m., I settle down with my second steaming cup of coffee and begin writing an articulate, abundantly brilliant motion to compel. Good for me. I pull out my "clock" time sheet and fill in the client's name and file number at 8:00 a.m., insert an appropriate, detailed summary of my task, and set off. I am cranking along just fine and am even able to combine time blocks by marking a straight line down from 8:00 a.m. to the next six minute increment while I'm toiling away on my motion, blissfully uninterrupted—a rare morning indeed.

But, it does not last. At 8:36 a.m. my paralegal, let's imagine him as the gruff, interrupting type (most of the good ones are), comes in with a letter for me to review and sign, knowing nothing of, and probably caring little about, my rigid clock regimen. I make some changes on it while he waits, and hand it back to him. It is now 8:39 a.m., and I set back to my motion. At 8:44 a.m., my phone rings—an eager client with a question. She asks me to pull up a draft pleading I sent her yesterday and make a few changes. It seems she has since been promoted and now has a new job title. Good for her. I make the changes and email the document back to her and set back to my motion. It is now 8:49 a.m., and my coffee is cold. But, more importantly, what is going on with my time sheet? How do I "stop the clock" at 8:36 a.m. and pick back up at 8:39 a.m. when my time sheet only allows for six minute increments? Do I round *up* for the letter revision? Round *down* for the motion work? And, what about the unproductive time spent worrying about this and filling in my time on that antiquated trap of a time sheet?

As you can see, the "clock" time sheet is simply unrealistic and unworkable. Trying to bill in time segments, *i.e.*, 10:00 a.m. to 11:00 a.m., will prove impossible. Rather, bill by the task performed and allot the appropriate time to it—1.0—regardless of the specific time in the day it was performed.

This is the practice of **task billing**. With task billing you bill the amount of time for tasks performed as opposed to identifying the specific time in the day that you spent on the file, *i.e.*, 8:36 a.m. to 8:42 a.m.

As you work up a file, there will be a litany of things you will do — *i.e.*, "tasks" you will perform — write a letter, make a phone call, draft a pleading, etc. These are all individual tasks that you perform on the file that need to be billed individually. Sometimes they will be done in a single time segment, that is, an exceedingly rare thirty minutes of uninterrupted time you can devote to one file only. But, more often than not, they will be performed independently, at scattered times throughout the day, when you find a spare moment to click on or glance at something related to that case. Because it is impossible to go back and recall exactly what time you began (8:36 a.m.) and completed (8:42 a.m.) the task to come up with a quantity of billable time (0.1), instead you keep up with the *tasks* you perform (letter, phone call) and reasonably estimate the time you spent on each or bill it at the lowest increment possible: 0.1.

Let's see how this shakes out for my young, budding associate. He asked:

> ***So, let's say I get an email from the court with a pleading attached. I read the pleading and determine I need to send it to the client. I send it to the client via email and the client comes back immediately with a question, which I answer. When do I start and stop the clock on this?***

He is clearly eager, invested and wants to do it right. If he is my associate, I have an equal incentive to teach him just that — so, let's walk through it. This is a sample time sheet. You will see it time and again throughout this guide. It consists of three columns: (1) file information (file name and number); (2) the time spent performing the specific task; and (3) the task description.

	File	Time	Task
File name ← File number ←	Smith 18874	0.1	Receipt and review of court notification enclosing court-issued Notice of Service on Defendant Brown
		0.1	Receipt and review of Notice of Service from the Court showing service was made via certified mail on Defendant Brown on October 10, 2012
		0.2	Emails to/from Mr. Client enclosing the Notice of Service received on Defendant Brown and advising of his Answer deadline of November 10, 2012

Now, my eager associate may have performed all of these tasks over the course of a single time segment—let's say an hour—while he was also engaged in phone calls from other clients, several exchanges with his legal assistant, a lashing from an angry partner and a re-heated cup of coffee, but I highly doubt he had a full, uninterrupted twenty-four minutes to devote solely to the Smith file. So, I instruct him to put a placeholder on his time sheet for each task he performs, as he performs it, and reasonably estimate the time spent on each task later or bill it at point-one.

A what?!?

A placeholder. Don't worry. I will teach you. You'll spend a tenth of the time you previously did preparing your time sheet. Keep reading.

Ahhhh . . . the notorious point-ones

0.1

You may hate them now because they do not seem to add up to much, but you will learn to utilize them. I had a very wise partner tell me once: "Did you know that there are over 80 point-ones in a day?"

Her comment baffled me at first because, when I did the mental math, to me there were over 100 point-ones in a day. I soon learned that's because she, as Older, Wiser Partner, had earned the right to work only eight hours a day, whereas I, as Young Lowly Associate, worked ten on a regular basis. But, despite the mathematical discrepancy, I was still stumped by the comment. I was not quite sure what it meant. *So, there are a lot of point-ones in a day? That's just math.*

Then, as I became a little older (and a little wiser myself) I finally put two and two together and realized she was trying to encourage me to bill more point-ones. As a new associate, I am sure most of my time entries back then ranged from five to six hour blocks for tasks described generically as "legal research" or "prepared motion." My partner was trying to teach me to break my time entries up into smaller segments with more detail, and it turned out to be sage advice. Try, as often as you can, to break down tasks, dissect them and bill them in smaller increments, as opposed to big, block batches. Why? It fulfills your ethical requirements to prepare detailed time entries that clearly show the work you performed. What's more, clients and courts hate block billing. In fact, you will find many corporate clients have made it a policy to reject outright and refuse to pay for any block-billed time.

Sample from Client Billing Guideline:

Task descriptions must include an itemization of each activity: *i.e.*, a detailed descriptions of each task performed in single-activity time entries, including the date on which it was performed and who performed it, that person's rate, the time expended (in 0.1 hour increments) and the charge for each task. General descriptions of work are not acceptable.

Single-activity tasks in 0.1 hour increments—that is the goal.

BILL IN BITES NOT BLOCKS

A court must be able to evaluate the hours expended, which means that attorneys must avoid vague billing entries and block billing for work that is performed.

Lindy Bros. Builders, Inc. v. Am. Radiator & Standard Sanitary Corp., 487 F.2d 161 (3d Cir. 1973)

I can't imagine why you would want to block bill, anyway. It shortens your time entry descriptions, which is never the goal and often leads to less tasks billed — also, never the goal. Here is an example of a block bill:

File	Time	Task
Smith 18874	0.5	Prepared letter to defense counsel discussing settlement offer; emails to/from Mr. Client enclosing draft letter for review/revision; made changes requested by Mr. Client; finalized and sent letter to defense counsel; email to Mr. Client enclosing copy of correspondence sent for his file

While the travesty in this example is pretty clear (there are five separate billable tasks in there—*five!*), sometimes it is not. Block billing can be a hard habit to break, but I will give you a hint. A tell-tale sign of a block entry is a semi-colon; entries with semi-colons are typically block bills. If you are writing the description for a time entry, and you feel the need for a semi-colon or a period, that is a sure-fire sign you are probably billing more than one task in a single entry. Do not do it. The goal is to bill *single-activity* tasks. A time entry should not require more than one sentence because it describes only one task.

Another tell-tale sign of a block-bill is more than one significant action verb—such as draft, review, correspondence to, revise, prepare, compile, etc. If your entry has you both reviewing some records and drafting a memorandum summarizing them, that's a block bill. If you revise a pleading then send it in an email to the client, that's a block bill. If you prepare a motion for summary judgment and then compile the exhibits to be filed in support, that's a block bill. The action verb can be a very valuable trigger for you to break the time entry up into two, if not more, time entries to ensure you are billing for a single task with each entry.

> ***Block billing is billing 'such that multiple tasks are aggregated into one billing entry thereby 'imped[ing] the court's efforts to evaluate the reasonableness of any of the listed activities.'***
>
> *Lindy Bros. Builders, Inc. v. Am. Radiator & Standard Sanitary Corp.,* 487 F.2d 161 (3d Cir. 1973) (internal citations omitted)

That block-billed entry should be broken up as follows:

File	Time	Task
Smith 18874	0.3	Prepared letter to defense counsel advising of client's decision to decline $15,000 settlement offer and provide no counter at this time
	0.2	Emails to/from Mr. Client enclosing draft letter to defense counsel declining $15,000 settlement offer for review and comment
	0.2	Revised letter to defense counsel declining $15,000 settlement offer to incorporate Mr. Client's comments and suggested revisions and finalized same for executing and sending
	0.1	Email to defense counsel enclosing letter declining $15,000 settlement offer and requesting response to same
	0.1	Email to Mr. Client enclosing executed copy of correspondence sent to defense counsel declining $15,000 settlement offer for his file

Win-Win.

Fee applicants should not 'lump' several services or tasks into one time sheet entry because it is then difficult if not impossible for a court to determine the reasonableness of the time spent on each of the individual services or tasks provided . . . .

Handschu v. Special Svcs. Div., 727 F. Supp. 2d 239, 249 (S.D.N.Y. 2010) (quoting *Williams v. N.Y. City Housing Auth.*, 975 F. Supp. 317, 327 (S.D.N.Y. 1997))

Now each task is broken out and separately billed in small, bite-size increments, resulting in a clearer, more itemized and detailed description of each phase of the settlement process. This will negate any potential question from the client or court concerning how you spent your time and will result in increased billing for you.

TIPS

CLIENT INVOLVEMENT

Note in the previous sample that I have referenced, highlighted almost, the client's involvement in the work product. It always helps to remind your clients that your billables are a product of your interaction with them and inclusion of their input in the legal strategy of the case. It is much harder for clients to gripe about bills that clearly show they were tugging on your ear and that you listened, responded, and included their input in the work product.

DESCRIPTION OF CONTENT OF LETTER

In the block bill sample, the letter at issue was described merely as a letter involving "settlement negotiations." This will prove highly inadequate. As you are likely aware, just like any other aspect of a case (discovery disputes, for instance), "settlement discussions" between you and opposing counsel may span the course of two weeks and five letters. If you describe each one as merely a letter involving "settlement discussions," your client may question the five seemingly identical entries on your bills. Make it clear that each of the five letters involved different phases of the settlement discussions, i.e., the initial offer, a decline and counter, a counter to the counter, etc. By simply adding the descriptor, "declining the $15,000 offer," that letter then becomes a uniquely purposeful, separately identifiable settlement letter among five, allowing you to bill clearly and conclusively for each.

THE "TO/FROM" ENTRY

Note the "to/from" entry in the sample prior. Perhaps this is the one exception to block billing, technically, because it does lump two separate tasks — both the "to" communication and the "from" — together, resulting in the 0.2 entry. While I have just instructed you to avoid block billing ("Break it up!"), breaking up quick back-and-forth, "to/from" exchanges into two separate entries ("Email to the client enclosing Complaint," "Email from the client confirming receipt of Complaint") may be a bit overkill. For this reason, I have combined them, but this is the one exception! This works as well for lengthy correspondence to/from the client on the same topic. If, in the course of one day, you and Mrs. Client send five or six emails back and forth analyzing and discussing the $15,000 settlement offer, you should collapse all of those into one "to/from" entry, noting the fact that it was lengthy to support the time allotted it, as follows:

File	Time	Task
Smith 18874	0.5	Extensive exchange of emails to/from Mrs. Client discussing the defendant's $15,000 settlement offer and Mrs. Client's optimal response to same

PREPARED VS. DRAFTED

It is an on-going debate, but, to my older, allegedly wiser partner's dismay, I prefer the word "prepared." Thus, in the previous sample entry, I use the phrase "Prepared letter" as opposed to "Drafted letter." It sounds more formal and also allows you to bill for the preparation of different drafts of a document. "Drafting a draft," just does not have the same ring to it.

FORMAL NAMES

In the sample entry on the previous page, notice how Mr. Client is called "Mr. Client," not "the client," a vague reference to him as just one of your many other clients, or "Robert A. Client, IV," his full birth-given name. Mr. Client strikes the right balance of specifically identifying him as the client contact with whom you were communicating while maintaining the appropriate degree of professionalism. Mr. or Mrs. Last name should be used when referring to the regular client contact as it will inform the person reviewing your bill both that you were engaged in billable work because you were interacting with the primary client contact and that your work involved attorney-client communications.

DESCRIPTIVE TITLES

You will note in the previous entry, defense counsel is not referred to by Ms. Last name, but, rather, by a descriptor: "defense counsel." For players other than your constant client contact, last name reference alone will likely not be sufficient. This is especially true if your client is a large, conglomerate corporation, Corporate Client, Inc. if you will, and your bills are reviewed not by your primary contact—someone with whom you discuss the case daily—but, rather, by a clerk in the legal department, who takes small pleasure in cutting your bill. When referring to people other than your primary client contact, with whom you speak and interact during the course of the litigation, use descriptive titles such as "defense counsel," "Corporate's causation expert," "the plaintiff's daughter," "Corporate's medical records director," "plaintiff's treating physician," etc. This will avoid any question as to how your communications with these individuals translate to billable work on the file.

Here are some other common tasks you may have been inadvertently block billing:

Drafts

Typically, when you sit down to prepare a motion or brief, the first draft you create is just that — a *draft*. It is usually sent to your partner and/or the client for review and comment. You read over it several times. You consult with others on it, and you revise it and refine it multiple times before it ever becomes remotely close to a 'final draft.' That is part of the process. You need to bill for it — as follows:

File	Time	Task
Smith 18874	1.2	Prepared first draft of Motion to Compel Defendant Brown's bank records
	0.3	Emails to/from Mrs. Client enclosing first draft of Motion to Compel Defendant Brown's bank records for initial review and comment
	0.4	Revised first draft of Motion to Compel Defendant Brown's bank records to incorporate Mrs. Client's comments and suggestions
	0.7	Review of applicable federal court law to support additional legal argument for financial disclosure of Defendant Brown's bank records
	0.8	Further review and revision of first draft of Motion to Compel Defendant Brown's bank records to add additional legal argument for financial disclosure and convert same into final draft for client review
	0.2	Emails to/from Mrs. Client enclosing revised Motion to Compel Defendant Brown's bank records for final review and approval for filing
	0.4	Final review of Motion to Compel Defendant Brown's bank records and formatted same for electronic filing with the court

NOTE the reference in the previous sample to the first draft of the motion as such, a "first draft," the email to the client requesting "initial comments and review," and the description of follow-up revision as "further review and revision." This makes it clear there was a separate draft version of the motion that was used for review and comment. It was then subsequently revised and edited before it became the final product. Note also the brief summary of the additions made ("adding the argument for financial disclosure") and the notation of the second email to the client as one requesting "final review and approval for filing." This, too, makes it clear what changes were made to differentiate the second draft from the first and demonstrates to the client that the second exchange involved final revisions and approval for filing rather than initial review and comment.

Adding/Revising Legal Arguments

In the prior sample entry, you will notice the description of the additions made to the motion during the second round of revision and review. I documented for the client what the revision entailed, *e.g.*, the adding of "additional legal argument for financial disclosure." This is far more descriptive than a generic "further revision to motion," which tells the client nothing about the revisions I made or how they enhanced the final product. With the short five-word descriptor of the legal argument added, the client now knows, specifically, what I added at this stage of the revision process, as opposed to the next and the next. This ensures I have adequately documented each phase of the process for the client and precluded confusion or question that

> *Counsel should make a good-faith effort to exclude from a fee request hours that are redundant.*
>
> *Hensley v. Eckerhart*, 461 U.S. 424 (1983)

would have certainly followed had I included several redundant entries on my bill simply for "further revision to motion."

Legal Research

If you break legal research up by topic and purpose it will enable you to bill separately for the various phases of legal research you perform on a file. For example, let's say you are working on a summary judgment motion in a products liability case, and you spend a few hours researching several different legal arguments you plan to assert in the brief. Do you think your client would prefer a bill that looks like this?

File	Time	Task
Smith 18874	7.4	Legal research for summary judgment motion

I certainly would not. I am not paying that bill, at least not without question and, perhaps, not without a fight. This, on the other hand, is a bill I can trust:

File	Time	Task
Smith 18874	2.7	Reviewed and compiled state court opinions finding misuse of product equates to contributory negligence in preparation for arguing same in summary judgment brief
	1.9	Reviewed and compiled federal court opinions supporting pre-emption of federal manufacturing standards over state law in preparation for arguing same in summary judgment brief
	2.8	Reviewed and compiled state court opinions concerning proper calculation of lost wages in preparation for arguing same in summary judgment brief

The premise is simple. Break it up.

> ***Use of broad categories such as "legal research," "interviews," "other services," or "review of files" do not prove to the court a reasonable expense of time without further explanation of the services provided.***
>
> *U.S.A. v. Thompson*, 361 F.Supp. 879 (D.C. 1973), aff'd in part, vacated in part sub nom, *U.S.A. v. Boggins*, 489 F.2d 1273 (D.C.Cir. 1974).

Preparing Separate Sections of Substantial Briefs

This is particularly applicable to motions for summary judgment, *Daubert* motions, and appellate briefs, which often require extensive work on separate sections of the brief. Often the all-intimidating "Narrative Statement of Undisputed Facts" takes loads more time to prepare than the argument section, particularly when it is an issue you have dealt with before and have plenty of well-crafted legal argument already to pull from. The facts section, however, will be different in every case. It will always require an exhaustive review of the 'world' of documents generated by your case, be it medical records, police reports, contracts, invoices, inspection reports, photos, depositions, etc., and preparation of a succinct, focused summary of the relevant facts at issue, each with a separate citation to the record. It is just going to take some time.

Rather than billing 8.5 hours for the global project ("Drafted motion for summary judgment"), segregate out the separate sections of the brief as follows:

File	Time	Task
Smith 18874	1.3	Reviewed and compiled relevant documents, records, depositions and pleadings in preparation for drafting Narrative Statement of Undisputed Facts for brief in support of summary judgment motion
	1.9	Prepared first draft of Narrative Statement of Undisputed Facts for brief in support of summary judgment motion with supporting citations to the record
	0.9	Further review and revision of first draft of Narrative Statement of Undisputed Facts to ensure accurate record citations and finalized same for client review
	1.4	Reviewed and compiled applicable state law to support legal argument for entry of judgment based on lack of standing for argument section of brief in support of motion for summary judgment
	1.8	Prepared first draft of Law and Argument section of brief in support of summary judgment arguing for entry of judgment based on lack of standing
	0.2	Emails to/from Mrs. Client enclosing first draft of brief in support of motion for summary judgment based on lack of standing for initial comment and review

You have now provided the client with a well-documented itemization of each phase of your preparation of the summary judgment brief, allowing the client to see the variety of tasks and stages involved. No client likes to see 8.5 hours spent on any one task. *Ever*. Trust me. It makes them picture you leaned back at your desk, latte in hand, staring dreamily out the window all day while you flip through a magazine and languorously ponder their case. Segregated billing invokes a much more productive image and also educates the client on the actual amount of work it takes to prepare an articulate, effective motion that is capable of obtaining judgment in their favor. Also note, as outlined in the previous bullet point, that the sample entry involves the preparation of the first draft only, not the further revisions the brief will inevitably undergo, as well as the necessary exchange with the client before it becomes a final draft, worthy of filing.

Medical Records Summaries

A detailed summary of all of the medical records involved in a case is usually a necessity, particularly in medical malpractice actions, but also in any case where the development and treatment of the plaintiff's injuries is an issue. When, in a personal injury case, is that not an issue? Rather than submit a bill to the client with a block, forty-hour entry for "Preparation of medical records summary," break your work up into two phases—first, the compilation and review of the records, and then the preparation of the timeline or summary. Also note timelines created for different purposes, *i.e.*, different admits, different providers or different signs, symptoms or treatment. Let me give you an example. Let's say you are handling a medical malpractice case involving a right knee injury and the corrective surgery your client performed. You will likely have records from a number of different medical providers leading up to the surgery, pre-surgery/consult records from your client, the orthopedic surgeon's office, as well as the hospital records from the surgery and post-surgery recovery and care. Rather than a forty-hour entry for "preparation of a medical records timeline" for review and summary of all of those records, break up your work as follows:

File	Time	Task
Smith 18874	0.9	Compiled and reviewed records from Plaintiff's pre-surgery visits with various providers relating to pain in the right knee in preparation for preparing summary of same
	1.1	Prepared summary of Plaintiff's pre-surgery visits with various providers documenting pain in the right knee
	0.8	Compiled and reviewed records from Dr. Smith's office relating to Plaintiff's visits prior to the October 4, 2005 surgery for treatment of pain in the right knee in preparation for drafting timeline of same
	1.4	Prepared detailed timeline of Plaintiff's visits to Dr. Smith's office prior to the October 4, 2005 surgery for treatment of pain in the right knee
	1.2	Compiled and reviewed records from Carraway Hospital from Plaintiff's October 4, 2005 admit for right knee surgery in preparation for drafting summary of same
	1.9	Prepared summary of Carraway Hospital records from Plaintiff's October 4, 2005 surgery on the right knee
	0.7	Compiled and reviewed records from multiple providers for Plaintiff's post-surgical care of the right knee and follow-up treatment, therapy and recovery of same
	1.2	Prepared detailed summary of records from multiple providers documenting Plaintiff's post-surgical care of the right knee and follow-up treatment, therapy and recovery of same

This sample described preparation of four separate summaries. However, whether you end up with one document which serves as a conglomerated master summary that allows for ease of reference on all admits, conditions and treatment described above or four separate timelines for each separate admit, condition, etc., break the billing up regardless to provide the client a more detailed summary of the various phases of work you performed in condensing the entirety of records into an efficient, workable timeline/summary that you and anyone else working on the file with you, including the client, can use for the duration of the matter through trial.

Reviewing Documents Produced in Discovery

Review of documents produced in discovery is crucial. You need to get your hands wrapped around the world of documents that comprise your case, and you need to go through them all—the relevant ones in excruciating detail, and the not-so-relevant ones in big skim batches, at least, to make sure there is no smoking gun. Either way, you have to lay eyes on all of them, and you need to properly bill for it. If a document-rich, corporate defendant dumps four thousand documents on you in response to discovery requests, rather than billing a hefty eight hours for "Review of documents produced by defendant in discovery," break your review up based on the different types of documents produced and, if possible, include a specific reason and goal for the review.

File	Time	Task
Smith 18874	1.4	Receipt and review of pre-1999 contracts produced by Defendant Company in response to discovery requests to assess pre-1999 terms of business between the parties
	0.5	Receipt and review of Fleet Operator Agreement produced by Defendant Company in response to discovery requests in preparation for 30(b)(6) deposition of Defendant Company
	0.9	Revised outline for Defendant Company's 30(b)(6) deposition to include questions relating to the Fleet Operator Agreement produced by Defendant Company in discovery
	2.3	Receipt and review of all parts invoices produced by Defendant Company in response to discovery requests in preparation for drafting timeline of pre-1999 purchases
	1.8	Prepared detailed timeline of pre-1999 purchases from invoices produced by Defendant Company for use as demonstrative aid at trial

This is much like the medical records review. You are simply breaking the review of thousands of documents up into specifically purposed, separately itemized tasks.

NOTE Much like the "compile and review" entries in the medical records time entries, the "receipt and review" entries here, noting the receipt and review of the documents, are segregated out from the entry describing whatever task was performed as a result of the document review, *i.e.*, preparation of a timeline, outline or memo to the file summarizing the documents, etc. You should always try to create some tangible work product from your document review—be it a summary, a timeline, notes, etc., but break it down. Create an entry for *review* of the documents in preparation of creating the work-product, whatever that may be, and a separate entry for *creation* of the timeline/memo/summary. Ask yourself: Why are you reviewing the documents, and what task did you perform as a result of your review?

Answer those questions in the form of two separate, itemized entries.

> ***Nearly all of the entries showed only one undivided total amount of time on any one date . . . [I]t was the plaintiffs' burden to show that the amount of time expended was reasonable, and this showing could not properly be made without some breakdown as to the separate functions performed and the number of hours devoted to each.***
>
> *LeRoy v. City of Houston*, 906 F.2d 1068 (5th Cri. 1990)

Note the Page Length of Voluminous Records

If a batch of records you need to review is particularly lengthy (thousands of pages) explain this in your time entry, including the number of pages, so the client will understand why it took you a substantial amount of time to review those records.

File	Time	Task
Smith 18874	3.2	Receipt and review of voluminous (3,456) page production in response to subpoena to Clark Construction

Compiling Documents to Produce

Ahhh . . . the rounding up of your client's documents to respond to discovery. Isn't that fun? But, we have all had to do it, and we have all had to deal with the problem-child client that likes to give you only what they *think* is relevant, regardless of what you ask for and tell them you need. But, the good news is, you can bill for it. And, as with everything, it is best done in stages, and with adequate descriptors:

File	Time	Task
Smith 18874	1.4	Receipt and review of invoices from Mrs. Client from 2002-2006 in preparation for organizing and compiling same for production in response to discovery requests
	0.6	Prepared memorandum to the file summarizing the invoices from 2002–2006 provided by Mrs. Client for use in discovery production and trial
	1.3	Organized invoices from 2002–2006 provided by Mrs. Client, redacting any confidential and/or non-discoverable information in preparation for producing same in response to Plaintiff's Requests for Production
	0.3	Final review of bates-stamped, production copy of 2002–2006 invoices provided by Mrs. Client and finalized same for production in response to Plaintiff's Requests for Production

This will also enable you to bill separately for different types of documents you review and compile in response to different requests — the invoices, here, as opposed to contracts or purchase orders or accounting records or what have you. This will also ensure the bill you submit for your hard discovery work is itemized and broken down, rather than a lump 40 hours for "review of documents for production." I am not paying that bill without a fight either.

TIPS

MEMO TO THE FILE

Note the entry in the previous sample for preparation of a memorandum to the file summarizing the invoices. Any time you find yourself knee-deep in documents, your head wrapped solidly around the dates, the symptoms, the amounts, or whatever other relevant information you are gleaning from your review, write it down! Tap out some rough summary of that relevant information while it is fresh on your mind and makes sense. It will save you a lot of time later by putting you immediately back there, in that keen state of intimacy with the documents, without having to repeat a painstaking or even cursory review.

The memo to the file will also make your truncated, condensed knowledge available for others—your partners and staff, even the client—and it produces a tangible product from your review, i.e., proof you did the work. A quick memo to the file is just good practice, particularly when it comes to document review, and will result in an additional billable task performed—the review, and then the memo. Again, win-win.

FINAL REVIEW

Just as you do with pleadings you file, i.e., review them one final time before filing, you do the same with documents you produce in discovery. That is, you look over them one final time before they are produced to make sure the bates-stamping is correct, the documents are in the right order, they are the redacted version if there was redacting and they do not contain any items that are not supposed to be produced. Make sure you are billing for this final review. Notice how I refer to the final copy as the "bates-stamped, production copy" to specifically identify it as the final copy, the one that is going out the door to that mustache-twirling attorney down the road. This separates it out from the original documents I initially reviewed and the organized, final batch I put together for bates-stamping. Bill everything in organized, well-documented phases.

THE SMALLEST TIME INCREMENT

One final lesson on block-billing. I cannot stress this enough. 0.1 is the smallest time increment for billing. If you are ever asked as a general policy to round all tasks up to 0.2 or told the smallest increment of time you are to bill is fifteen minutes or more, do not do it. It does not accurately or ethically reflect the amount of time you spent on the task and it can result in the denial of a fees request by the court.

Kronfeld v. Transworld Airlines, Inc.,
129 F.R.D. 598 (S.D.N.Y. 1990)

> *Finding firm's practice of increasing the minimal billing increment to 0.25 hours, even for one-minute and five-minute telephone calls, resulted in entries "well in excess of the actual time spent on many of the calls."*

Ecos, Inc. v. Brinegar,
671 F.Supp. 381 (M.D.N.C. 1987)

> *Court was convinced that firm's practice of rounding all entries up to multiples of 15 minutes meant the time records did not "accurately reflect the amount of time actually expended on the case."*

BILL MORE TASKS

I am not a betting man, but I would like to wager that if you and I sat down and discussed your typical day, I could point out at least ten things you did that you did not bill for. Why? Because to you, they probably just seem like mundane things that you always do as an attorney: review and revision, checks and double-checks, organization of records, hand-off instructions, etc. Just a typical part of your routine.

Not billable, *per se*. Wrong. Ask yourself, why are you doing these things? *Why?* Because they ensure your pleadings are accurate, your filings are correct, your file is organized, efficient, useful, and that you are moving your client's case forward — the most important part. These tasks ensure you are giving your client solid representation. You need to bill for them, but many do not.

Here are some of the most glaring omissions I have encountered:

Compile and Review

Note that for each timeline in the sample medical records entries there are two separate entries: (1) one for the compilation and review of the records; and (2) another for the preparation of the timeline/summary of the records. Any time you do anything with documents, you first have to pull together whatever batch of documents you are going to review (which might be a substantial task) before you can review, summarize, analyze or do whatever it is you plan to do with them. Be sure you are being compensated for that time with a separate, itemized entry. And, if you can state in that entry the purpose of the review, *i.e.*, "in preparation for drafting timeline of treatment of right knee pain," that is helpful as well. While it is clear to us as lawyers that we need to review, at least briefly, all records that come in on a case, it may not be as clear to the client, particularly *why we* need to review them. Educate the client with your invoices. Provide the answer to that question up-front, on your invoice, and avoid any question or curiosity from the client later concerning extensive document review.

Review of Exhibits

Any time you receive a motion for summary judgment or discovery motion or just about any pleading these days, they will come with exhibits attached. Those take time to review. A 1.7 entry for "Review of Defendant's Motion for Summary Judgment" is a bit harder to swallow than the following:

File	Time	Task
Smith 18874	0.9	Receipt and review of Defendant's Motion for Summary Judgment along with supporting brief and narrative statement of undisputed facts
	0.8	Receipt and review of Exhibits filed in support of Defendant's Brief in support of Motion for Summary Judgment, *i.e.*, the disputed contracts, invoices, discovery responses and Defendant's Affidavit addressing these items

This is particularly true if the exhibits are lengthy, which they often are. If that is the case, *i.e.*, the exhibits opposing counsel attached to his motion are 300 pages long, break your review of them up and bill them separately, just as you would with review of documents produced in discovery. Meaning, you segregate out your review of the (1) contracts, (2) invoices, (3) discovery responses, and (4) defendant's affidavit addressing these items into four separate time entries. If the entire pleading, including exhibits, was 350 pages, your client is going to prefer itemized entries as opposed to a block-billed, four-hour task.

Client Review and Input

Many clients are very involved in your motion practice. They want to see drafts, revise and critique them, in other words, assert themselves in the work product. Great, fantastic, the more the merrier! While I am sure that is not what you find yourself thinking as they are telling you where to put commas, the good news is, again, at least you can bill for it:

File	Time	Task
Smith 18874	0.3	Emails to/from Mrs. Client enclosing first draft of Motion to Compel Defendant's profit and loss statements for initial review and comment
	0.8	Revised Motion to Compel Defendant's profit and loss statements to incorporate Mrs. Client's input and suggestions
	0.2	Emails to/from Mrs. Client enclosing final version of Motion to Compel Defendant's profit and loss statements for final review and approval for filing with the court

Some clients even require you send them draft pleadings for review/approval before filing. Particularly if the client is requiring it, you should be billing for it:

Sample Client Billing Guideline:

All briefs in support of motions must be received in our offices five days before service of same is due upon opposing counsel in order to permit the [Client] file supervisor an opportunity to review and discuss the brief prior to service and filing.

Final Review and Finalization

Every attorney worth his salt reads back through his motion one last time before filing to make sure it is accurate, free of typos, to check that the style, certificate of service and date are correct and that the exhibits are all organized and marked correctly. The question is not whether you performed this task. I am going to trust you did and do, every time. The question, rather, is whether you bill for it. Many do not. You will now:

File	Time	Task
Smith 18874	0.3	Final review and revision of Corporate Client's Motion for Reconsideration and finalized same for filing with the Court

Selection of Exhibits

This is one I believe many attorneys miss. In drafting that brilliant pleading, you had to sift through the relevant documents and decide which ones should be attached as exhibits, did you not? Some must be attached because you need them to be part of the record. Some should not be attached because they are not supportive or not relevant. Some should be redacted or otherwise truncated before they are filed with the court. Those decisions all translate to work on your part. Make sure you are billing for it:

File	Time	Task
Smith 18874	0.3	Selection and compilation of exhibits, *i.e.* the loan documents, account history printout and check copies, to be filed in support of Corporate Client's Complaint against Defendant Brown

Receipt of Court Notifications

Did you receive an email from the court notifying you the plaintiff filed something? Did you click it open immediately to see what was filed? Even while you were at home, kicked back on the couch? Of course you did. We all do. If you are going to *work* after work, at least make sure you bill for it.

File	Time	Task
Smith 18874	0.1	Receipt and review of electronic notification from the court enclosing plaintiff's Motion for Temporary Restraining Order

Formal Names of Pleadings

Note in the previous sample entry (and in every entry used in this guide that involves a pleading) the formal name of the pleadings is used, and it is capitalized.

Meaning, the motion plaintiff filed is not referenced in your times sheet merely as "TRO," or "motion for TRO," or even "motion for temporary restraining order." It is "Plaintiff's Motion for Temporary Restraining Order," appropriately titled and capitalized as if it were a defined term. This may seem a little too informal to you, but it makes your bill look proficient and professional. If I had to guess, I bet you would rather show up to a barbeque in a blazer than to a formal dinner in shorts and flip flops. As is always the case in communications with the client — it is better to err on the formal side.

Abbreviations in Time Entries

While we are on this topic, I do not advocate the use of standard abbreviations, such as TRO, MSJ, MTD, MTC, etc., in your bills to clients. While some clients may know what these mean, some may not, so it's best not to get in the habit. Language used to describe tasks in bills should have the same degree of formality as would be used in written correspondence to the client — formal and professional. And, feel free to disagree if you like, but some clients may not invite you back to their next formal dinner in those flip-flops.

Let us also not lose sight of the obvious here.

Time spent explaining your bill to the client is not only uncomfortable, it is also not billable. Make your bills clear, detailed and self-explanatory at the outset and you will save yourself more time to perform more billable tasks that move the case forward rather than put it into a stalled argument over your invoices.

Court Notifications for Your Own Filings

Here is one you may not have thought of: Did you receive an electronic notification from the court after your paralegal filed your motion? Did you click it open immediately to make sure he titled the pleading correctly and noted the proper filing party? Did you open the pleading and scroll through it quickly to make sure it was the right pleading, the right version and that the exhibits were marked and scanned into the court record correctly? The answer to this question is likely the same—even at home, even while on the couch. Of course you did. We all do. You trust your paralegal, but you are always going to check behind him to make sure your pleadings are filed correctly. That way, if there is an error, you can fix it immediately. In other words, you do this to be sure the pleadings you file on behalf of your client are scanned, indexed and noted in the court record correctly. As the attorney, that is your job. Make sure you are billing for it.

File	Time	Task
Smith 18874	0.1	Receipt and review of electronic notice from the court confirming receipt of Corporate Client's Motion for Summary Judgment and indexing of same in the court record

Prep Time

This is one of the worst omissions I have seen. Every time you go to a hearing, or go meet with a doctor or expert or witness—every time—you prepare for it. Typically, you compile the relevant pleadings, documents or records you will need for the hearing/meeting, you review them, and then prepare (either mentally or on paper) a rough outline for your oral argument or line of questioning for the meeting/hearing. At the very least, you take a moment to wrap your mind around the legal arguments and issues involved so you can speak coherently about them. You prepare, so bill for it.

File	Time	Task
Smith 18874	0.5	Compiled and reviewed Motion to Compel lost wage information and related pleadings in preparation for hearing before Judge Johnson on same
	0.3	Prepared outline for oral argument before Judge Johnson on Corporate Client's Motion to Compel lost wage information

File	Time	Task
Smith 18874	0.7	Reviewed and organized Plaintiff's records from August 4, 2009 Emergency Room visit in preparation for meeting with ER Physician, Dr. Smith, who treated Plaintiff on August 4, 2009
	0.5	Prepared memorandum to file summarizing Plaintiff's records from August 4, 2009 Emergency Room visit and outlining questions for use in meeting with ER Physician, Dr. Smith, who treated Plaintiff on August 4, 2009

File	Time	Task
Smith 18874	0.7	Compiled and reviewed cases cited by defense counsel in its Motion for Summary Judgment in preparation for hearing before Judge Johnson on same
	0.5	Prepared memorandum to file summarizing the cases and legal arguments cited by defense counsel in its Motion for Summary Judgment for use in opposing same at hearing

File	Time	Task
Smith 18874	0.6	Compiled and reviewed Corporate Client's expert appraiser's appraisal report in preparation for meeting with Mr. Smith to discuss his valuation opinion
	0.9	Prepared outline summarizing Corporate Client's expert appraiser's appraisal report and setting forth questions to ask Mr. Smith during meeting tomorrow to discuss his valuation opinion

Note Taking

Did you scribble down some relevant dates when reviewing defendant's employment records, some relevant symptoms when reviewing plaintiff's medical records, some relevant figures when reviewing defendant's tax returns?

I am sure if you wrote it down, it was because it will be useful to the case. Be sure to preserve the information to the file and bill for it. You can type them up, dictate them for your assistant to put in memo form, or just scan your handwritten notes to the file in pdf format and give the document a search-worthy title, *i.e.*, "Plaintiff's back treatments in 2006," so you and others working on the file will be able to easily locate it later and benefit from the condensed information. Also, for those with phones smarter than they (I know mine is), if you are generating notes remotely, at an inspection site, perhaps, or while meeting with a witness or doctor, in addition to your handwritten notes, use your phone to take pictures of anything relevant you come across while you are there (*i.e.*, a warning label on the product at issue, a sign by the bathrooms cautioning about a wet floor, your client's employee badge). Later, be sure to save the photo to the file with accompanying explanation, date the photo was taken and a search-worthy title, *i.e.*, "Wet Floor Sign from Site Inspection 5.7.2022," thereby converting the information into usable memoranda for the file. And, as always, be sure to bill for it. Here are some examples:

File	Time	Task
Smith 18874	0.4	Prepared memorandum to the file from review of defendant's employment records outlining dates defendant was unemployed
	0.8	Prepared memorandum to the file from review of plaintiff's medical records outlining instances where he complained of lower back pain
	0.7	Prepared memorandum to the file from meeting with defendant's accountant outlining income received from his business from 1998-2002
	0.3	Prepared memorandum to file identifying manufacturer, date of manufacture and warning labels on the subject saw

Thinking About a Case

I think, therefore I bill. It is true. As an attorney, you are paid not for physical labor but for your mental ability, your legal thought processes. For better or for worse, the practice of law is a mental profession; meaning, it has its benefits (you can do it anywhere) but, also, its consequences (you tend to do it anywhere—in the evenings, in the middle of your sleep, even when you are on vacation). It is just the nature of the beast. But, if you spend concrete time—five minutes here, a half-hour there—truly contemplating your client's case, the issues involved, the strengths and weaknesses, and the best way to reach your client's goal, you need to bill for that. It is that kind of mental labor that your client is paying you for. But, I am sure that is giving you heartburn. No one wants to start an entry with "Thought about x, y, z . . ." That gives me heartburn, too. Never do that. Rather, document it as "Evaluated strategy for responding to plaintiff's Motion to . . .". Or, better yet, build it into the time spent on whatever task it was that prompted your thoughts about the case. If you spent fifteen minutes last night considering an additional argument for the motion to compel you are drafting today, be sure to add that time to today's motion to compel time entry. If you spent five minutes in the shower this morning deciding whether to omit or include that last legal argument in your motion for summary judgment, add that time to today's motion for summary judgment entry. And so on.

Had a bright idea?

Great! When considering something new, that you cannot tie to a billable task (because it is not one you performed, but merely one you considered), try these entries:

File	Time	Task
Smith 18874	0.6	Researched methods to obtain Plaintiff's employment records from Bill's Hardware Store and potential cost of each for discussion with Mr. client concerning same
	0.4	Researched likelihood of success of lack of standing argument to determine whether to include same in motion for summary judgment
	0.5	Reviewed and considered various legal arguments to establish Plaintiff's lack of personal jurisdiction and the likelihood of success of each
	0.6	Researched and considered potential arguments to prevent Defendant Brown from obtaining Mr. Client's customer lists for discussion with Mr. Client concerning same

Discussion with the Client

Note in the last entry in the previous sample that the "research" and "consideration" were undertaken specifically for a "discussion with the client concerning same." This is helpful if you spend a good bit of time merely considering a certain legal strategy. And, know that you *should* spend a good bit of time merely considering an argument if it is a complicated legal argument and there are costs and benefits of asserting it. Do NOT be afraid to spend time simply thinking about your cases. You are a lawyer; that is your job. However, if you do, it may be a good idea to involve the client. Send the client an email giving a summary of your thoughts, some research if you conducted it, the pros and cons and your conclusion, and ask for their input. The client will likely appreciate the fact that you are actively thinking about his case and will engage. This will also ensure no question about your bill later when you included time entries for "research" and "consideration" because the client was actively involved in your legal thought processes. He will know, from your tangible reports and requests for input, that you were hard at work considering the best legal strategy for his case. Be sure to bill for your time spent: 1) requesting authority from the client to file something, 2) receiving and/or discussing said authority; and 3) any changes the client requests in the pleading or strategy.

Physical Appearances Require (at Least) Three Parts

Anytime you attend a physical event (hearing, deposition, out of office meeting, inspection, etc.) you should have at least three time entries generated as a result of the event. Start with the pre-event preparation. Maybe you compiled the relevant cases or exhibits and reviewed them. Maybe you made an outline of your argument or questions you wanted to ask. Anytime, as a lawyer, you are going to a physical meeting of such importance you're going to take steps to prepare, even if it is just mentally, but it will likely also involve the creation of tangible work product as well. Those are your pre-event tasks. Then, of course, you attend the event. That is a task. Then, post-event, you should always notify the client of how things went. This could be done in an email or over a phone call and, if the latter, should also be memorialized in writing in a letter. You may also jot some notes to the file summarizing key facts or takeaways from the event. At the very least, any physical event should generate three time entries: 1) the pre-event preparation; 2) the event; and 3) the post-event work and debrief.

Missing tasks?

Feel like you have done more than your time sheet is giving you credit for? You probably have! You are probably letting valuable tasks slip through the cracks by inadvertently omitting tasks you performed from your time sheet. Here are some tricks to avoid it:

Your mailboxes

Sent Emails: Scroll back through your sent emails. You will undoubtedly uncover tasks you performed, but in the stress and clutter of the day, you may have forgot to bill for.

E-File Notices: Conduct a search of your emails for e-file notices from the court. This will likely remind you of pleadings

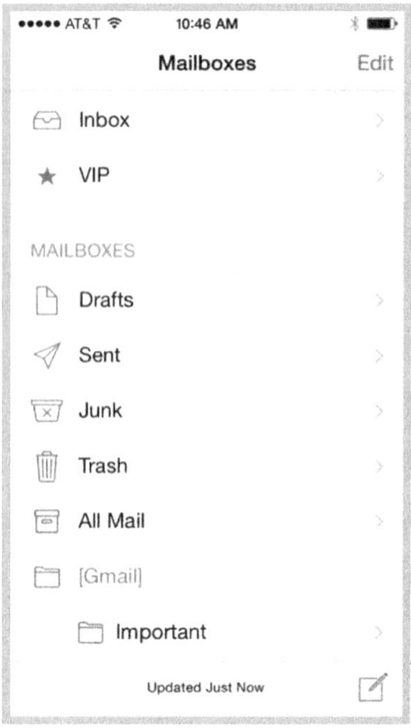

you filed, received, reviewed or downloaded, that need to be included on your time sheet.

Inbox: The same applies to your inbox. As you are finishing your time sheet for the day and putting placeholders on your time sheet for the next day, a good place to check for tasks that need to be completed before you leave as well as upcoming tasks you need put on your timesheet for tomorrow is your inbox.

Your calls

Same goes for your recent calls. If you can review calls made on your office phone, scroll back through them. Or look through your recent calls on your cell phone. There may have been a quick exchange or two that you forgot to bill.

Your stacks

Let's face it. We all have them. The ever-present "stacks" on our desk. Flip through them to see if there is any work you accomplished on those projects that may not have made it to your time sheet that day. Doing this at the end of every day will also help you jot down tasks you need to complete the following day on your time sheet which now doubles as your to-do list.

Your case list

Go through it at the end of the day. You will likely uncover billable tasks you need to perform or, at the very least, ensure you are up to date on all deadlines and needs of the case.

Send the client an update: Often attorneys, because they are working upwards of 30–40 cases, can forget how time may feel like it's dragging for the client on the other side, for whom this may be the sole and single time she's been involved in litigation. For the client, receiving an email from their attorney, even a simple short one providing an update, is often greatly appreciated. So, not only is this another task you can perform and bill for, you can also pat yourself on the back for keeping your client updated and informed.

Call one person on every case once a week: This will not only increase your billable hours but also improve your case management and communication skills. It can be easier than you think, as a budding attorney whose case list is growing, to lose sight of the particular needs of each case. If you have fifteen minutes at the end of your day, scroll through your case list to make sure there aren't any glaring deadlines or tasks uncompleted that you need to focus on and pick up the phone to follow up on these outstanding items or upcoming deadlines to keep your case moving forward.

"This is to confirm" letters: "This is to confirm" letters solidify discussions that need memorializing but only took place in a spoken communication. Think back through your day for any important conversation that took place. Perhaps you spoke with the client on strategy for producing redacted documents. Tap out a quick "this is to confirm" letter. It will serve as another billable task and will ensure that client's file is documented with the legal strategy you both decided upon. These types of letters are also often needed for important agreements made with opposing counsel, *i.e.*, for extensions of deadlines, agreements on documents to be produced, or confirmation that everything has been produced, agreements not to object to certain lines of questioning or documents to be admitted, etc.

Avoid big block bills by touching multiple cases each day: Think of your case list like a lazy Susan. At least once each day—and particularly on days where you've devoted most of your working hours to one monstrous task in one particular case—give your case list "a spin" and touch a new case. This helps to let your mind get a rest, too, from whatever deep research, brief, or issue that is consuming you in another matter. A "fresh look" can sometimes be all you need to find that missing argument or perspective that was killing your argument yesterday. Let a mental break devoted to a different case and client help you reset.

BILL IN MORE DETAIL

While you do not want to write a novel for each entry, it is always better to err on the side of caution and include more detail than less. Worst case scenario is your partner may gripe about having to read too much when reviewing your bills or the client may ask for more succinct entries, but you'll certainly never be asked how you spent your time on the file. The latter inquiry is far worse than an overly detailed bill, trust me. Less can be more, but, to start out, more is more. You can always cull it down later if asked or if you feel the need, but you cannot sculpt without clay. It

Courts may deny compensation where the billing information submitted is "too vague to sufficiently document the hours claimed."

Grievson v. Rochester Psychiatric Ctr., 746 F. Supp. 2d 454, 466 (W.D.N.Y. 2010); *see also* *Tatum v. City of N.Y.*, 2010 WL 334975 at *7 (S.D.N.Y. 2010) (quoting *Kirsch v. Fleet St., Ltd.*, 148 F.3d 149, 172 (2d. Cir. 1998))

Clients want more:

Sample from Client Billing Guideline:

Generic descriptions or work are not acceptable and will not be processed for payment.

is best to get it on the books at the outset so it is clear the tasks you performed on the file, and their purpose, then edit later if necessary.

This guide is filled with plenty of sample time entries you can use, but here are some tasks that often benefit from a little extra description:

Legal Research

Did you do some extensive research for a summary judgment motion? Congratulations! Good work. But, I hope this is not your entry:

File	Time	Task
Smith 18874	3.2	Legal research for summary judgment motion

As the client, I can tell you I am certainly going to question that bill. I discussed previously how to break legal research up into different topics for different legal arguments in your summary judgment brief, but also be sure you tell the client in the task description where you were researching, what you were looking for and why? Those are answers I cannot glean from this meager, six-word entry ("Legal research for summary judgment motion"). The description for legal research should always be just that: descriptive.

The client wants to know:

- What is the specific topic you are researching?
- What is the goal of your research?
- What legal arguments are you trying to find and where do you plan to assert them?

Excerpt from Client Billing Guideline:

[Client] assumes that the attorneys selected for the representation team possess the requisite knowledge of the general legal concepts associated with the issues existing in the matter. Research shall be related to a specific issue(s) and shall not be of a general or background nature.

Always try to throw in 5–8 words about what it is you researched, what database you searched in, and the goal of your research. Rather than the vague, non-descript entry above ("Legal research for summary judgment motion"), try this instead:

File	Time	Task
Smith 18874	3.2	Reviewed and compiled state court opinions finding establishment of ownership based on adverse possession to support argument for same in summary judgment motion

That's much better. *"Terry, please put this bill in line for payment. Thank you."*

"Opinions" Not "Cases"

Note in the previous sample entries the mention of compilation of "opinions" as opposed to "cases." It just sounds more formal, more professional. Also, some clients may not know exactly what other "cases" are. Review of opinions, as opposed to cases, is more universal and more readily recognizable as legal research.

"Reviewed and Compiled"

Notice the phrase "reviewed and compiled" in the previous sample entry. I am sure when you conduct legal research, you either print cases and summarize key language or (more likely) you are cutting and pasting relevant quotes from the cases you review online and saving them to a Word document that you can easily convert to the legal argument section of your brief later on. This is the basis for the "compiled" notation. You compiled the relevant information (legal quotes) into a workable format (case summaries) to help you prepare the brief. You will undoubtedly refer back to these case summaries and quotes to help you prepare the brief. If so, you have created useful, tangible work product for the file. Congratulations. Be sure you are billing for it:

File	Time	Task
Smith 18874	3.2	Prepared memorandum to file summarizing relevant state court law on establishment of ownership through adverse possession for use in motion practice and trial

Communications

Always, always, include a few words describing the content of your written communications, both those that you "receive and review," and those that you "prepare." Why? Because it tells the client specifically which communication you are billing time for and distinguishes it from other letters, calls and emails on the same topic that you will undoubtedly have to engage in and subsequently bill.

Also, as a side note, if you are ever required to submit your invoices to the court for review to support an entry of attorney's fees (as we all must on occasion), including both a description of the content of your communication in addition to the "to/from" indicator allows you to prove attorney-client communications were made while maintaining the privilege by redacting the content, as follows:

File	Time	Task
Smith 18874	0.3	Emails to/ from Mrs. Client concerning Plaintiff's $15,000 settlement offer

File	Time	Task
Smith 18874	0.3	Emails to/ from Mrs. Client concerning *[redacted]*

File invoices under seal

When submitting invoices to the court to support a request for attorney's fees always (always!) file a motion for leave to submit the invoices under seal. Anything filed with the court becomes public record. Allowing all the legal world, particularly your competitors, access to your invoices, showing them the tasks you bill for, your task descriptions, the hours you bill, your rates, etc. is never a good idea. You made a wise decision to purchase this guide and sharpen your billing skills. Protect your investment. File a motion for leave to file your invoices under seal, highlighting to the court the "commercial, sensitive and proprietary nature" of your bills. Most judges — having once practiced as private attorneys themselves — are intimately familiar with the sensitive nature of legal bills and will readily grant the request. You will find a sample Motion for Leave to File Under Seal in the Appendix to this guide. (**See Appendix A**).

Affidavit to establish reasonableness of fees

Also, when filing a motion with the court to recover attorney's fees, it is helpful to submit an affidavit — from either the senior partner on the file, *i.e.*, the attorney with the most experience in that area of the law, or an attorney outside the firm in the local community experienced in that area of the law — establishing the reasonableness of the hours and rates charged. Some courts may award attorney's fees without such an affidavit but many will not and the reasonableness of the fees should be proven before they can be recovered. So, protect your own record and submit an affidavit that establishes:

1. The affiant's experience in that particular area of the law;
2. Her familiarity with rates other lawyers in the communicate who actively practice in that area charge;
3. The hours and rates your firm charged (attaching invoices with privileged, attorney-client communications redacted); and
4. Her belief that the hours and rates charged by your firm are reasonable.

A sample Affidavit establishing reasonableness of fees is included in the Appendix to this guide. (**See Appendix B**).

Not just details. Valuable details.

One last detail tip. As lawyers, we know every word we write should have purpose and intention. No words should be superfluous. The most important goal you can accomplish with a detailed time entry is to show the client how you are adding **value** to the case. What does the task you completed accomplish? How does it move the case forward to resolution? This is the value. And, this is an easy way to remember how to construct your time entries to fulfill this goal.

A.T.V.
Action. Thing. Value.

Think about the *reason* you are performing the task and try to work that into your time entry to educate the client on the value of your services. Some examples:

- Why are you preparing that Motion to Dismiss? To seek dismissal based on plaintiff's lack of standing. *Put that in your time entry.*
- Why are you writing opposing counsel? To request an extension of defendant's discovery production deadline. *Include that in your entry.*
- Why did you attend that hearing? To argue in opposition to plaintiff's motion to compel. *I know you are getting this.*
- Why are you preparing that subpoena? To obtain plaintiff's orthopedic medical records. *See? Much more helpful to the client.*
- Even depositions, particularly when they are not of the main parties to the case, can benefit from some valuable explanation. Why did you notice and attend that non-party witness deposition?

File	Time	Task
Smith 18874	1.7	Attended deposition of eyewitness Ms. Sims to scrutinize her account of the accident

Incorporate the "why" — the *value* — where you can in your time entry to remind the client that your goal is not to simply do busy work so you can bill hours, but, rather, to always move their case forward to resolution.

BILL BY GUIDELINES

Many corporate clients, particularly those that defend claims nationwide and employ lawyers in a number of different states, often have their own billing guidelines for local counsel. They will usually send a copy of their guidelines to you with the request for engagement and condition your representation of the company upon your agreement to abide by their billing guidelines. This is the client's way of asking you to accept their "terms and conditions" before proceeding. So, what do you do? Agree, of course! We all do. But, the question is, do you actually read the guidelines?

All the way through?

The client wants to know.

And I say that not because it is the prudent, mature thing to do. We are lawyers, but that does not mean we are prudent and mature 100% of the time. But, in this case, a thorough review of the client's billing guidelines will help you tailor your bills to the client's needs and preferences to ensure payment. We are lawyers. We all want to get paid 100% of the time.

Also, as a young attorney, the number of hours you write on your time sheet matters none if it is not time your partner can bill to the client. Reading your client's billing guidelines will ensure you are spending your time doing tasks that are billable and crafting time sheets your partner can translate to billable earnings for the firm.

Here are some other benefits to knowing your client's billing guidelines:

Learn What the Client Will Not Pay For

Most client billing guidelines will include a list of certain tasks and items the client simply will not pay for. Why else have guidelines, if not to tell their attorneys what they can and cannot bill for?

Sample Client Billing Guidelines:

Non-Reimbursable Fees

[Client] will not pay or reimburse the outside counsel firm for the following types of fees submitted on an invoice:

- Unproductive travel time for lawyers or paralegals.
- Time spent preparing bills.
- Greater than the firm's out-of-pocket cost for temporary lawyers or paralegals retained for [Client] matters.
- IT support or administrative tasks like loading files to databases. Any exceptions to this policy must be pre-approved by [Client].
- Paralegal, secretarial, or clerical overtime or for HVAC (heating, ventilating, and air-conditioning) charges.
- Duplicate entries on an invoice or across several invoices.

- Scheduling a review of firm personnel.
- Conflict checking.
- Preparation of budgets of time, staffing, or total costs of projected legal work.
- Time associated with the compliance with these practices and procedures or to any legal audit, either internal or external, of bills and expenses.
- Summer associate time.
- Computer time other than the actual to the firm of computer-assisted legal research and where the requested research is agreed to by [Client].
- Multiple attorneys, law clerks, and paralegals "educating" themselves on the case. We will also not pay for "training" or "apprenticeship" time.
- Time opening or closing files.
- Excessive reviewing of a file by multiple time-keepers.
- Fees older than 120 days, unless otherwise approved or an alternative agreement has been provided.
- Time spent by a new member of the firm's team getting up to speed, unless approved in advance.
- Attendance at seminars, continuing legal education, and conferences.

I know. Quite a few, right? But, do not worry. With the techniques you have learned in this guide, you already know how to avoid a great number of those (duplicate entries, clerical time, excessive review, etc.). You likely were not planning on charging the others to your client. HVAC charges? Probably not.

And, you certainly will not now that you have read the client's billing guidelines. Having done so, you will have avoided any unpleasant exchange with your client or senior partner over entries for non-billable time, as well as any excuse that clerk in the billing department may have concocted to cut your bill. She likely keeps her own worn, dog-eared set of the billing guidelines right next to her scissors. Don't give her the pleasure.

Learn the Client's Task Codes

Many clients will require you to assign certain task codes to each task you perform or they will not pay the bill, at least not without issue.

SAMPLE TASK CODES

L210	Code L200: Pre-Trial Pleadings and Motions. Subset L210: Pleadings.
L220	Code L200: Pre-Trial Pleadings and Motions. Subset L220: Preliminary Injunctions/Provisional Remedies.
L230	Code L200: Pre-Trial Pleadings and Motions. Subset L230: Court Mandated Conferences.
L240	Code L200: Pre-Trial Pleadings and Motions. Subset L240: Dispositive Motions
L250	Code L200: Pre-Trial Pleadings and Motions. Subset L250: Other Written Motions/Submissions.

Avoid the issue on the front-end by learning the codes and training yourself or your assistant to enter the appropriate codes with each task.

Include the proper code designations for each task on your time sheet entries to ease entry of the time into the system and payment and processing by the client.

	Smith 18874 Codes:	Prepared Brief in Support of Corporate Client's Motion for Summary Judgment based on Plaintiff's lack of sufficient expert opinion on causation
Task Codes: →	L240	
→	L230	Prepared Motion for Summary Judgment in favor of Corporate Client based on Plaintiff's lack of sufficient expert opinion on causation
→	L250	Prepared Motion to Strike Plaintiff's causation expert, Dr. Smith, for lack of sufficient credentials and qualifications to testify as to the cause of Plaintiff's damages
→	L230	Attended pre-trial conference before Judge Johnston to argue Motion to Strike Plaintiff's causation expert and other motions *in limine* in preparation for trial

This way the bill is presented to the client in the precise manner they need to put it in line for payment.

> ***Moreover, taking the time to read the client's billing guidelines and ensure your bills match precisely the format the client has requested not only ensures ease of processing and payment, it also reminds the client of your professionalism and attention to detail, traits that they will now be confident you employ on the same level when handling their legal matters.***

Uncover More Billable Tasks to Perform

This is the real benefit of thoroughly reviewing your client's billing guidelines. You will often uncover additional billable tasks that the client wants you to perform, meaning more billed hours for you. Most clients (at least ones large enough to use billing guidelines) require interim status reports at specific intervals and on specific forms set forth in their billing guidelines.

Sample Client Billing Guidelines:

I. REPORTING PROCEDURES

Initial Evaluation

a. [Client] requires an initial evaluation as to damages, range of exposure, liability assessment of the court, judge, and jury panel, and a summary of proposed future investigation or discovery within thirty (30) to ninety (90) days of receipt of the assignment. These evaluations should include a report of the deposition of the plaintiff, whenever appropriate. Included in the evaluation must be estimated costs for fees and expenses.

II. STATUS REPORT

a. This is a one page report that must be completed by local counsel in conjunction with their much more detailed six month litigation updates. The purpose of the status report is to:

1. Provide currently available information.
2. Provide an overall picture of the litigation at that moment in time.
3. Provide a roadmap of what needs to be done in the future.

Status Report Form:

ATTORNEY STATUS REPORT FORM

CAPTION:

File No.:
Date of Accident:
Insured:
Co-Defendants:
Description:

Plaintiff:
Jurisdiction:
Court:
Plaintiff's attorney:

INVESTIGATION AND DISCOVERY:

Investigation complete?:
If no, suggested investigation:

Discovery complete?:
If no, outstanding discovery:

INJURY AND SPECIAL DAMAGES:

Injuries:
Lost wages:
Other:

LIABILITY:

Is this a case of liability?:
If so, why?:

Probability of winning:

SETTLEMENT CHRONOLOGY AND EVALUATION:

Demand:
Offer:
Recommended offer:
Range of verdict:

LITIGATION COSTS:

Fees to date:
Disbursements:
Estimated prep. costs:
Estimated trial costs:

COMMENTS:

Attorney:

Date:

III. 90 DAY PRE-TRIAL REPORTS

a. Ninety days prior to any potential trial, [Client] must be provided with a full written evaluation of the case. Such evaluation should include the liability and damage aspects of the case, credibility of all witnesses, including experts expected to testify (both plaintiff and defense), with a brief summary of their expected testimony, identification of significant legal issues, and applicable case law and motions (including appropriate motions in limine), and an appraisal of plaintiff's attorney and the trial judge.

Of course you were going to keep the client informed and updated on the status of the matter as the case progressed, but now you know the client wants you to prepare written, detailed status reports at particular intervals in the litigation. These are particularly billable tasks. Thus, reading and abiding by the client's billing guidelines translates to more billable work for you, not to mention impressed and satisfied clients for the firm. Win-win.

BILL ONLY BILLABLE TASKS

As demonstrated in the previous chapter, there are just some tasks certain clients will not pay for. Some very important CEO or board of directors met at one point in time, took a vote, and decided there were some things they simply never wanted to see again on a legal bill. Good for them. Don't let that deter you. Perform tasks you *can* bill for, and get compensated for your work.

It is also important to remind yourself that time spent appealing rejected time is not billable. Meaning, if you spend .5 hours appealing 1.0 of rejected time, your best outcome is a loss of only .5 hours of work — that you could have been putting toward billable tasks that progress your cases. But, a worse outcome would be a denial of the rejection, resulting in a loss of 1.5 hours of your work. Your time would be more wisely spent becoming a wiser biller by studying your client's billing guidelines and learning what is billable and what is not, that way you don't waste any time billing non-billable tasks.

Here are a few common examples of tasks some clients deem non-billable.

TRAVEL

So, the client has decided they will not pay for travel. Alright. Do not bill for travel then. To the extent possible, spend whatever portion of that time you can performing *billable* tasks on that file that you can put on your time sheet.

That way, what was once:

File	Time	Task
Smith 18874	~~0.6~~	~~Travel to Orange County for hearing before Judge Johnston on Motion for Summary Judgment~~
	1.1	Attended hearing in Orange County before Judge Johnston on Motion for Summary Judgment
	~~0.6~~	~~Return travel from Orange County for hearing before Judge Johnston on Motion for Summary Judgment~~

Becomes:

File	Time	Task
Smith 18874	0.4	Review of Motion for Summary Judgment and related pleadings and prepared outline for oral argument for hearing on same
	1.1	Attended hearing in Orange County before Judge Johnston on Motion for Summary Judgment
	0.2	Meeting with opposing counsel following hearing on Motion for Summary Judgment to discuss status of case and related discovery matters
	0.2	Telephone call to Judge Johnston's clerk to discuss preparation of a proposed order for entry of summary judgment
	0.2	Telephone call to Mr. Client to report on this morning's hearing before Judge Johnston on Motion for Summary Judgment and discussion with opposing counsel after the hearing

If you performed these tasks during the time you were traveling, title them by the billable tasks that they are and reclaim the previously non-billable time.

TIPS

Note in the previous sample entry the "meeting with opposing counsel." Any time you go to a hearing to argue a motion and opposing counsel is present, you will likely take a moment or two to discuss the case with her. "Did you get those documents I sent you?" "Does that date work for you for the deposition?" "Are you going to file a motion on that?" It is brief, sure, but nine times out of ten you will have some meaningful exchange, albeit brief, about the case. Be sure you are billing for that.

You always report to the client after a hearing to let them know how it went. Even if it is just a quick email or call to tell them you argued the motion and the court is going to take the matter under submission, that is a point-one. And, if it is a back-and-forth exchange, point-two. See? I told you these point-ones were going to start adding up. Stick with the program. The program works.

INNER-OFFICE MEETINGS

In addition to travel, the client has also informed you they will not pay for time you spend in inner-office meetings. That enlightening, eye-opening hour you spent with Senior Partner Saul hashing out all of the pitfalls and benefits of that new legal argument you came up with over the weekend, *i.e.*, whether it will work for the client and, if so, when it should be asserted and the potential consequences of your position. All of that good, solid legal work that will surely result in a win for the client, does not impress them. They are not paying for it. While I get it, in part, I do—the client does not want to pay double time, both you and Senior Saul's, for you two to sit, feet kicked up on the conference table in high-back leather chairs, mentioning their case only briefly while you spend the remainder of the hour discussing last night's game (or that's at least how the client might imagine it).

> *But, oftentimes, a quick chat with a senior partner on an area of the law you may be new to, but that he has dealt with for twenty years, is exceedingly valuable to the client. The costly hours it would have required for you to get a handle on that area of the law, and the even more costly errors you might have made in the process, in order to acquire the wealth of knowledge and experience you gained from Saul in that half-hour conversation, is well worth it. If you feel you gained some insight or guidance from the meeting that will enhance your representation of the client, find a way to memorialize the information. You can likely conduct some quick research now confirming Saul's theory in half the time because you know the buzz words and key terms to search for. Pull together some legal authority supporting Saul's theory, prepare a quick memo to the file summarizing it and draft an email to the client outlining your thoughts and insight, etc. This way, you can convert what was previously non-billable time—an inner-office meeting—into billable tasks—research, memo, email.*

So, what was once "non-billable" time that the client would surely cut from your bill:

File	Time	Task
Smith 18874	~~0.7~~	~~Meeting with firm's real estate attorney, Saul Jones, to discuss optimal method to prevent bank foreclosure on Mr. Client's property~~
	1.1	Prepared first draft of Temporary Restraining Order to prevent foreclosure of Mr. Client's property

Becomes time spent doing billable work, *i.e.*, researching and strategizing the optimal pursuit of the client's goal:

File	Time	Task
Smith 18874	0.5	Researched optimal method to prevent foreclosure on Mr. Client's property and procedure for same
	0.2	Emails to/from Mr. Client discussing best legal defense to foreclosure action and preparation of a Temporary Restraining Order to prevent same
	1.1	Prepared first draft of Temporary Restraining Order to prevent foreclosure of Mr. Client's property

Let the client benefit from the collective knowledge of your firm in the form of billable tasks that memorialize the information and help progress their case.

See Francis v. Atlantic Infiniti, Ltd., 34 Mic. 3d 1221 (Sup. Ct. Queens County, 2012) (wherein the court noted that the excessive time spent by the lead attorney may have been avoided had he been provided the support, guidance and supervision of the firm that would have represented the firm's collective experience).

BILL MORE PARALEGAL TIME

Be sure your paralegals are also billing for all billable tasks performed. In the same vein, be sure your assistant, if she performs paralegal tasks, bills her paralegal time as well. Know that some clients will require you to identify all paralegals that will perform work on a file as part of the engagement process, so be sure you identify your assistant at this phase if you expect she will perform billable tasks on the matter. Also be sure to train your staff to craft their entries for paralegal time in such a manner as not to appear clerical as most clients, and courts, will not pay or award fees for "clerical" work.

Richardson v. Byrd, 709 F.2d 1016 (5th Cir. 1983) (declining to award paralegal work that could have been performed by secretarial personnel)

Let's go through some common examples:

Compiled Materials for a Hearing/Meeting

Did your paralegal prepare a binder of materials for your summary judgment hearing? Make sure he bills for it.

File	Time	Task
Smith 18874	0.3	Searched online court docket, compiled pertinent pleadings and prepared files for Attorney Smith's use at summary judgment hearing

NOTE this entry applies equally to meetings, depositions, interviews, etc. Anytime your paralegal prepares a binder or folder of materials for your use at a hearing, meeting, interview, deposition, etc., he should be billing for this task.

Also, be sure your paralegal is using appropriate words to describe his paralegal tasks and avoiding terms that makes his work appear clerical:

SECRETARIAL	PARALEGAL
"Made copies"	"Compile and prepared files"
"Put records in binders"	"Organized key medical records"
"Printed cases"	"Retrieved relevant legal authority"

Enclosure Letters

Letters simply enclosing a pleading to the client are often considered secretarial and non-billable. Meaning, if your paralegal prepares a letter to the client enclosing, let's say, an order denying the plaintiff's motion to compel certain discovery materials, a time entry saying "Prepared letter to client enclosing Order Denying Plaintiff's Motion to Compel" will likely be cut as a secretarial enclosure letter. Don't get deterred. Get educated. If the letter really is that basic, perhaps the client is trying to send you a message. *Only bill me for tasks of substance that progress the case forward.* Heed the lesson. Train your paralegals to draft more than just an enclosure letter. Add a few sentences explaining what the enclosed pleading means and what the next focus in the case will be. They should be sufficiently steeped in the case and law to explain what a pleading means.

Imagine your paralegal drafted a letter far more valuable to the client like this:

> Dear Client:
>
> Enclosed you will find the Court's recent Order Denying Plaintiff's Motion to Compel. Plaintiff was seeking to compel us to produce the comments Mr. Sanders, our engineering expert, prepared that accompanied the photos he took during the second inspection of Plaintiff's property. Judge Drake denied the motion, which means we do not have to produce the comments. We are currently focused on preparing the Motion for Summary Judgment and will send you a draft for your review before filing. If you have any questions or wish to discuss the case further, please do not hesitate to reach out.

That's a fine letter. That's not simply a cover letter. It is now a *status* letter that informs the client. I would expect an entry like this for that standup paralegal work, an entry that would not fall prey to the same "enclosure letter" cut as the previous one-sentence letter would have.

File	Time	Task
Smith 18874	0.3	Prepared status letter to client explaining Court's Order Denying Plaintiff's Motion to Compel and discussing next steps

Scheduling

The same would likely apply to correspondence or phone calls spent solely on scheduling. Many clients would deem such a communication secretarial and not pay for it. The message: do more than the non-billable task. Train your paralegals to confirm all the specifics of a deposition or hearing in communications, *i.e.*, whether it will be in person or conducted remotely, whether it will be videotaped or whether a court reporter will be present, who all will be in appearance, how exhibits will be marked and handled, etc. This way the correspondence accomplishes more than simply scheduling, which is a better outcome for the client anyway in that it does more to move the case forward.

File	Time	Task
Smith 18874	0.3	Correspondence to opposing counsel's office to confirm AV and other technical elements of Plaintiff's deposition

I hope the goal here is clear. This is not simply a recharacterization of the task to make it billable. It is a response to the client's determination that the more basic task—enclosure letter, scheduling, etc.—is not billable and a choice to dive deeper, perform more than the basic task, and accomplish more as well, including payment for the time spent.

PUBLIC RECORDS SEARCHES

Secretary of State Searches

Did your staff log onto the Secretary of State's website to verify the registered agent for service on a corporate defendant?

File	Time	Task
Smith 18874	0.2	Reviewed Secretary of State records to identify Defendant Company's registered agent for service of process of the Complaint

PACER

Did your assistant access available PACER records to verify the defendant had not filed bankruptcy before you filed a complaint against him?

File	Time	Task
Smith 18874	0.2	Reviewed federal bankruptcy filings to ensure Defendant Brown has not filed bankruptcy to allow filing Complaint against him on subject debt

Probate

Did your paralegal search probate records to locate any priority liens on the plaintiff's property before you proceeded with foreclosure?

File	Time	Task
Smith 18874	0.4	Reviewed public records to locate priority liens on plaintiff's property before proceeding with foreclosure

Court Records

Did your paralegal search court records to compile background information on the plaintiff in preparation for her deposition?

File	Time	Task
Smith 18874	0.3	Reviewed state court criminal and civil records to locate any prior suits or filings against plaintiff in preparation for drafting memorandum to file summarizing same

NOTE In the sample entry prior, the research was conducted "in preparation for drafting memorandum to the file regarding same." If that is the case, be sure there is a corresponding entry for preparing the memorandum:

File	Time	Task
Smith 18874	0.4	Prepared memorandum to the file summarizing all prior civil and criminal filings against plaintiff for Attorney Smith's use in deposition and trial

Receipt of Court Notices

Notice the phrase in the previous sample entry, "updated case status chart." This ensures the entry does not register as clerical work (copying, filing, etc.) but, rather, as legitimate paralegal work in preparing a case status chart that ensures the file is always current, remotely accessible, and organized. A better file means better representation. If your paralegal is downloading pleadings and saving them to the file and preparing an accompanying index or other document that makes the pleadings readily available for viewing and/or preparing a chart or index of the pleadings for ease of use, he needs to bill for that.

Receipt of Documents

This same format should be used any time your assistant or paralegal receives records that need to be scanned into the file (which is, these days, pretty much any document that comes in): medical records, discovery production, correspondence, etc. The entry should reflect the "compiling and indexing" the recently filed pleadings and "updating the case status chart accordingly."

Receipt of Court Pleadings

If your state court e-filing system is anywhere near the twentieth century, your paralegal or assistant is probably copied on every email you receive from the court. While you do not want them billing for substantively reviewing these emails, your paralegal or assistant, if he is downloading the documents and saving them to the file or a pleadings index, he needs to bill for that:

File	Time	Task
Smith 18874	0.2	Receipt and review of order from court denying Defendant Brown's Motion to Dismiss, downloaded and indexed same to case status chart

Summarized Medical Records

Did your assistant or paralegal prepare a medical records timeline?

File	Time	Task
Smith 18874	0.4	Review of medical records from Plaintiff's November 5, 2009 admission to Carraway Hospital in preparation for preparing summary and timeline of same

And be sure, as outlined previously in the "Bill in Bites Not Blocks" chapter, that your paralegal does not submit a 40-hour entry for preparation of a summary of medical records. Just as you would, have him break up his entries into separate symptoms, dates, admits, conditions, etc. that he located and summarized in his timeline.

Prepared Case Calendar

Did your assistant or paralegal prepare a calendar for the case setting forth all upcoming deadlines, or perhaps enter these on your calendar for you?

File	Time	Task
Smith 18874	0.4	Receipt and review of general pre-trial order issued by the court and prepared case calendar outlining all discovery and motion deadlines for Attorney Smith's reference and use

These may sound like mundane tasks, but they are important. They result in a more organized, useful file for you and higher quality representation for your client. Your paralegal was likely doing most of these things already, but perhaps not billing for them. Now you will be sure he does. Here are some more examples of paralegal tasks:

File	Time	Task
Smith 18874	0.9	Reviewed Corporate Client's phone logs from September 1999 and redacted privileged attorney-client communications per Attorney Smith's request
	0.3	Compiled, organized and verified proper chronological order of September 1999 phone logs in preparation for bates-stamping of same for production in response to Plaintiff's Requests for Production

File	Time	Task
Smith 18874	0.2	Telephone call to Judge Jones' clerk to discuss deadline for filing response to Defendant's Motion for Sanctions per Attorney Smith's request

File	Time	Task
Smith 18874	0.3	Emails to/from defense counsel's assistant to coordinate scheduling of Defendant Brown's deposition and location and court reporter to be used for same

File	Time	Task
Smith 18874	0.3	Emails to/from Competent Court Reporting to schedule court reporter for Defendant Brown's deposition at defense counsel's office on May 23, 2011

File	Time	Task
Smith 18874	0.3	Final review of Motion to Compel Defendant Brown's deposition to verify all exhibits and the Certificate of Service and finalized same for filing with the court

Final review

Note the "final review" entry in the sample above. Like you, your paralegals should also conduct a "final review" of pleadings before filing to check for typos, ensure all exhibits referenced in the pleading are correctly designated and attached to the pleadings, verify the accuracy of the Certificate of Service and the style of the pleading, etc. Even if it is only a point-one entry, this should be done regardless. Make sure your paralegal is billing for it.

File	Time	Task
Smith 18874	0.2	Emails to/from process server to discuss service attempts on Defendant Brown and potential need to file motion for service by publication
	0.2	Prepared letter to New York Press Register requesting Affidavit for Service by Publication for use in filing Notice of Service with the court to establish service on Defendant Brown
	0.8	Prepared draft Motion for Service of Defendant Brown by Publication attaching Affidavit of Service from New York Press Register for review by Attorney Smith

Draft Pleadings and Letters

Paralegals should bill for any time spent drafting basic, form pleadings (Notice of Appearance, Notice of Intent to Serve Subpoena, Notice of Filing, Notice of Deposition, etc.). However, these should always be prepared for "review by Attorney Smith." Likewise, you, Attorney Smith, should have a correlating entry for reviewing the pleading your paralegal drafted before filing, even if it is just point-one. This applies equally to letters your paralegal prepares for your review.

Also, note the professionalism and uniformity of these paralegal time entries. They mirror the numerous attorney entries you have seen in this guide wherein clients are referred to by formal name, as are attorneys (Attorney Lastname is optimal), pleadings are capitalized and treated as defined terms, the phrases "receipt and review," "compiled and organized," are used, etc. Review your paralegal's or assistant's time entries and teach them to write time entries that are sufficiently descriptive and professional in order to meet client approval. Better yet, buy them a copy of this guide and save your time for more billable work!

Client Billing Guideline

The invoice itself should include a chronological listing of professional time billed, specifying the name of each lawyer and paralegal, the hourly rate, and the work performed by category by each such professional. All charges for services by attorneys and paralegals must be recorded daily based upon their actual time.

BILL MORE BY KEEPING LESS

The bad news about billing is that it is not billable. All time spent preparing time sheets, reviewing bills, appealing rejected bills, etc. does not translate to money in your pocket. So, minimize it. Just as you would with any other administrative element of your practice that does not require your legal knowledge and training—delegate it. You need to spend your time flexing your legal muscles, researching legal arguments, drafting brilliant briefs, crafting impenetrable discovery responses, negotiating, strategizing, and the like. Your time is much better devoted to performing all of the tasks your client is really paying you for, not spending valuable hours filling out a time sheet. Delegate it.

So, how do you do that? It is simple. You turn it into a system, a process that is routine and can be learned and repeated and, thus, taught. For starters, I would highly recommend you not physically write your time down on paper. Type your time sheets using some kind of word processing program. Trust me, just do it. It is quicker, easier to edit, and can be cut and pasted. Better for all. But, if you do insist on handwriting, this system will at least allow you to write your placeholders and your assistant can then type in the polish language as she enters your time into the system. I know she will agree with me on this one. Typewritten time is better.

The words "placeholders" and "polish language" might be new to you. We will get there. Stick with me. So, this guide has taught you how to bill far more tasks that you were performing but not billing for and how to craft detailed, documented time entries that will satisfy the client and the court. You now know how to bill more, ethically. Clearly, it was money well spent. But, what you may not have noticed is that this guide also taught you how to make certain elements of your time entries uniform and repetitive so they can be repeated. By whom? Your gruff, hard-working assistant that is who. Compliment her, treat her well, and teach her how to help you bill more.

You will notice in all of the sample time entries included in this guide, we have used some phrases over and over and over again:

- Receipt and review of electronic notification from the court enclosing . . .
- Receipt and review of . . . and brief and exhibits filed in support of same
- Emails to/from Mrs. Client enclosing . . . and discussing same
- Reviewed state court opinions concerning . . . in preparation for drafting . . .
- Prepared first draft of . . .
- Compiled and organized documents to be filed as exhibits in support of . . .
- Emails to/from Mrs. Client enclosing . . . for initial comment and review
- Reviewed and revised . . . to incorporate Mrs. Client's comments and suggestions

- Emails to/from Mrs. Client enclosing revised version of . . . for final review and approval before filing with the court
- Final review and revision of . . . and finalized same for filing with the court
- Email to Mrs. Client enclosing a court-stamped copy of . . .

You have already seen entries that begin and end like this eight times over while reading this guide. You have probably started to glaze over when you read them because they look a bit like legalese. Great! That is the goal. They all look professional. They all look standard. That is what you want. All that is missing from the entries above is the content — what documents you were reviewing or sending and the substance of your communications concerning these documents — that is all you really need to focus on when you prepare your time sheet. While the repetitive, formal language in the descriptions above are necessary to adequately and professionally describe your work, they are not hard to replicate, which means you can draft the "placeholders" and delegate the "polish" to your assistant or paralegal.

Your time sheet, the paper or electronic document that you access frequently throughout the day to tap out quick descriptors of the billable tasks you perform (*as you perform them!*), need only consist of bare-bones placeholder entries, leaving the simple task of adding the "polish" language shown above to your assistant as she enters your time.

It helps to see this in action. Let's look at time entries for a summary judgment motion filed by the defendant and your preparation of an opposition to that motion. Your rough-draft time sheet for this work may look like the column on the left, while your assistant will magically (and easily) transform it into the formal, polished product on the right for billing.

Your "Placeholder" Time Sheet	The "Polished" Bill
R/R of e-notice for Def's MSJ	Receipt and review of electronic notification from the court enclosing Defendant Brown's Motion for Summary Judgment
R/R of Def's MSJ and exhs	Receipt and review of Defendant Brown's Motion for Summary Judgment, supporting brief and exhibits filed in support of same
E to client encl. Def's MSJ	Email to Mrs. Client enclosing Defendant Brown's Motion for Summary Judgment for review and discussion
LR state ct re: Def's contrib neg def in prep for Opp to MSJ	Reviewed state court opinions concerning the contributory negligence defense raised by Defendant Brown in his Motion for Summary Judgment in preparation for drafting Opposition to same
First draft of Opp to MSJ	Preparation of first draft of Corporate Client's Opposition to Defendant Brown's Motion for Summary Judgment
C/O exhs for Opp to MSJ	Compiled and organized documents to be filed as exhibits in support of Corporate Client's Opposition to Defendant Brown's Motion for Summary Judgment

Your "Placeholder" Time Sheet	The "Polished" Bill
E t/f client encl draft Opp to MSJ for cmt	Emails to/from Mrs. Client enclosing first draft of Corporate Client's Opposition to Defendant Brown's Motion for Summary Judgment for initial comment and review
R/R MSJ Opp to incorp client's cmts	Reviewed and revised Corporate Client's Opposition to Defendant Brown's Motion for Summary Judgment to incorporate Mrs. Client's comments and suggestions
E t/f client encl final MSJ Opp for approval	Emails to/from Mrs. Client enclosing revised version of Opposition to Defendant Brown's Motion for Summary Judgment for final review and approval before filing with the court
Final R/R of MSJ Opp for filing	Final review and revision of Corporate Client's Opposition to Defendant Brown's Motion for Summary Judgment and finalized same for filing with the court
E to client encl ct-stamped copy MSJ Opp	Email to Mrs. Client enclosing a court-stamped copy of the Opposition to Defendant Brown's Motion for Summary Judgment filed on behalf of Corporate Client

Note the brevity of the placeholder entries on the right. Think of how much time you will save tapping out those quick, "code" entries contemporaneously as you complete tasks, particularly point-ones, as opposed to writing out all of the pomp and circumstance on the right.

As an attorney, you have a duty to keep contemporaneous time records.

> *An attorney must maintain accurate records of work done and time spent in preparing for each client's case. An attorney's failure to keep books of account and other records could be a basis for disciplinary action.*
>
> *Marino v. Denevi*,
> 182 Cal. App. 3d 553 (Cal.App. 1986)

> *[T]he absence of detailed contemporaneous time records, except in extraordinary circumstances, will call for a substantial reduction in any award or, in egregious cases, disallowance.*
>
> *Grendel's Den, Inc. v. Larkin*,
> 749 F.2d 945 (1st Cir. 1984)

This system will ease that burden.

With placeholders, you will now spend a quarter of the time keeping up with your time. Sure, it looks like code, but it is not really that hard to decipher, particularly for attorneys and legal assistants that work together closely day in and day out and are familiar with the typical abbreviations (MSJ, MTD, MTC, Opp., Ltr., etc.). Plus, your assistant knows, generally, what pleadings, documents and discovery requests you are working on daily, because she is there in the trenches with you.

And, just look at it. You probably could have read the column on the left, as you sit here today, and wagered a pretty good guess for what those time entries stand for. It is not rocket science. Your assistant will simply know that any time you mention the client, she is to call her by her formal name. Anytime you mention a pleading, she is to call it by its formal name. Anytime you mention discovery, she is to say it is "in response to Plaintiff's Requests for Production" or whatever request you are responding to. And so on. She will pick up on the receipt/review ("R/R"), compile/organize ("C/O") abbreviations as you go along. But, teach your assistant to add these flourishes to your time entries, and save your time for performing more billable work. It may take some time for her to get used to your "code" but she will get there. The return on investment is worth it. Train her to be a valuable part of the team and the team will then be more valuable. Trust me.

Here are some more examples:

Your "Placeholder" Time Sheet	The "Polished" Bill
R/R of 2006 invoices from client for disc.	Receipt and review of 2006 invoices provided by Mrs. Client for production in response to Plaintiff's Requests for Production
C/O 2006 invoices for redact/bates	Compiled and organized 2006 invoices provided by Mrs. Client and redacted privileged/non-discoverable information in preparation for bates-stamping and finalizing of same for production
Ltr to PC declining $15k settlement offer	Prepared letter to Plaintiff's counsel declining $15,000 settlement offer

Your "Placeholder" Time Sheet	The "Polished" Bill
E to client encl ltr to PC declining $15k	Email to Mrs. Client enclosing copy of letter sent to plaintiff's counsel declining $15,000 settlement offer
R/R of purchase orders from Def in resp to our RFPs	Receipt and review of purchase orders Defendant Brown produced in response to Corporate Client's Requests for Production
Memo to file re: purchase orders	Prepared memorandum to the file summarizing the purchase orders produced by Defendant Brown in response to Corporate Client's Requests for Production
R/R of P's med recs from Carraway re: UTI	Receipt and review of Plaintiff's medical records from Carraway Hospital relating to her urinary tract infection
Draft Compl. against Brookwood - brch of K	Prepared draft Complaint against Brookwood Engineering for breach of contract

I could easily go on, but I think you can see how quick and easy it could be for you to come up with a workable "code" to enable your assistant to translate your bare-bones time sheet into professional, bill-worthy time entries. Train her. Teach her. Even make her a cheat sheet or legend if you need. Delegate the mechanical work to her and save your time for performing more billable legal tasks.

Don't have an assistant or paralegal?

Don't let that deter you. This method can be implemented even if it just you, your shingle, and a telephone. Use the placeholder entries during the day while you are performing billable tasks to preserve the information, at least in rough format. Then, go back at the end of each day (I would recommend you not let *one day* pass without your time being somehow converted into invoice format) and "polish" your entries so they are ready to be billed. This may take an additional half hour at the end of your day, but save that time for after close of business and use the quick, short hand during the day to accomplish more billable tasks during business hours.

Don't work in front of a computer?

Still not a problem. If you find you spend more of your billable time at depositions, inspections, meetings, in court or traveling, dictate time entries either on a portable recording device or as notes in your phone. You can then review them later when preparing your time sheet or send them electronically (via text or email) to your assistant or paralegal for entry into the system. Do whatever you have to do to capture the tasks contemporaneously so you do not lose billable time.

Don't like to type?

That is okay, too. Dictate! With the significant advances in technology today, you can easily dictate time entries for review later or send them electronically to your assistant. You can use a portable recording device, such as your phone, or there are also many outside sources these days that provide dictation services. You can dictate your time entries over the phone and receive an electronic document back to use for entry into the billing system. Anyone can do this.

The primary goal is for you to train yourself to keep up with tasks as you perform them, *i.e.*, contemporaneously. As you begin (or even think of!) tasks, jot placeholders down on your rough time sheet — *right then!* — to ensure you capture them. At the end of each day, you should have a completed time sheet ready for entry into the system, which accounts for all tasks performed that day and describes them in a manner to ensure payment by the client. Waiting until the end of the day, the next day — or worse — next week, to try and recall all of the tasks you performed, particularly the point-ones several days ago, is a sure-fire way to guarantee you will lose time, which means you will lose money. Train yourself to do it contemporaneously.

TIMEKEEPING SOFTWARE

When I first began practicing, some of my older partners thought it was quite "newfangled" that I decided to keep my time in a digital Word doc, rather than on an old school yellow legal pad. I can't imagine what they would think now of the many varied timekeeping software programs that are now available to attorneys. Remember, however, even if your firm has purchased and uses timekeeping software, the crafting of your time entries to ensure they are sufficiently detailed to meet your ethical obligations and state billable tasks only still falls on you.

One great thing about timekeeping software is that you can add time from anywhere, right to a cloud-based drive, to ensure no time goes missing due to a lost legal pad, or a Word doc that seizes up. It also may remove the additional step of your paralegal or legal assistant entering your time for you. Timekeeping programs can also auto-populate time entries (for you to modify accordingly) from your calendar events, tasks, communication logs, notes, and documents, which can be incredibly helpful.

You can also program in numerous shortcuts that the program will then automatically populate when it prepares the bill. For example, your time entry may read "tct" and the program knows that means "Telephone call to." This greatly truncates the time it takes you to enter your tasks, leaving you more time to perform more tasks and keep your cases moving forward.

Here are some more examples of helpful timekeeping software shortcuts:

"rcf"	becomes	"Receive correspondence from"
"tcf"	becomes	"Telephone call from"
"rae"	becomes	"Review and evaluate"
"oc"	becomes	"Opposing counsel"
"pl"	becomes	"Plaintiff"
"df"	becomes	"Defendant"
"msj"	becomes	"Motion for Summary Judgment"
"mtc"	becomes	"Motion to Compel"

Aside from the timekeeping time-savings a software program offers, primarily one of the most valuable components of timekeeping software is the ability it affords law firms to analyze both each attorney's hourly performance and the firm's performance as a whole. Partners often don't have reliable insights into how many hours their associates spend on different tasks and clients, and without that data, they cannot effectively control and correct inefficient, wasteful work and billing practices. This is where timekeeping software can play a vital role.

Timekeeping software can track what percentage of hours attorneys are working that are billed and those that are not, pinpointing areas where improvements can be made. Having a complete picture of key metrics related to hours worked empowers firms to make better and more strategic business decisions. Partners can view the data and not only decide which attorneys are more profitable, but also which clients as well by identifying those whose work requires more non-billable tasks or whose bills regularly come back sliced and discounted.

Without offering any endorsement as to a specific timekeeping software program, here are a few of the top providers in the industry:

CliO:	www.clio.com
Practice Panther Legal Software:	www.practicepanther.com
Zola Suite:	zolasuite.com
Smokeball:	www.smokeball.com
Filevine:	www.filevine.com/billing-and-timekeeping

CONCLUSION

I hope this guide has identified for you a number of tasks you were already performing but not billing and has taught you how to effectively bill each of them, separately and clearly, to negate client confusion and ensure payment. Even better, if this guide enlightened you to tasks you were not performing, but should, I have only given you more tasks to perform and bill for—you can thank me later by buying the third edition. At the very least, I hope this guide has provided you the tools necessary to spend less time keeping your time and more time performing billable tasks, resulting in increased hours and impressed partners and clients. Billing can be easier. Anyone can learn to bill more efficiently and effectively and bill more, ethically, with the tips and techniques outlined in this guide.

APPENDIX A

MOTION FOR LEAVE TO FILE UNDER SEAL

COMES NOW Plaintiff, Corporate Client, Inc. ("Corporate") and respectfully requests the Court grant it leave to file its Petition for Attorneys' Fees and Costs under seal. In support of this Motion, Corporate submits to the Court that the Affidavit of Senior Partner filed in support of its Petition and the invoices attached thereto, which Corporate is filing to support its claim for attorneys' fees in this matter, includes copies of invoices submitted to its client in this matter, discussion of the rates counsel for Corporate charges and the hours and time spent in litigating this matter. This information is sensitive and proprietary and vital to the continued business of Law Firm, P.C. and should not be made public. Attached hereto as **"Exhibit A"** and incorporated by reference for all purposes is the subject pleading to be filed under seal.

WHEREFORE, Corporate respectfully requests the Court grant its Motion for Leave to File its Petition for Attorneys' Fees and Costs and supporting Affidavit and invoices under seal to preserve the confidentiality and proprietary nature of same.

APPENDIX B

AFFIDAVIT OF SENIOR PARTNER

Before me, the undersigned authority, personally appeared Senior Partner, and having been first duly sworn, does depose and say as follows:

1. My name is Senior Partner, and I am a licensed, practicing attorney in Anytown, Anystate.
2. I am the primary attorney for Corporate Client, Inc. in the above styled action.
3. I have been practicing in the area of [*insert*] in Anytown for over fifteen (15) years. [*Also include any other special appointments, designations, awards, certificates, etc. Senior Partner may have obtained in her particular practice area here*]. I have extensive experience and practice in the field of [*insert*].
4. My associate, Adam Associate, who also worked on this file has been practicing with our firm in the area of [*insert*] for approximately five (5) years.
5. Other attorneys and staff in our office have also worked on this file and they each have extensive experience in [*insert*].

6. It is my opinion that the hours spent and the expenses incurred by my firm in representing Corporate Client, Inc.'s interests in this matter were reasonable.
7. Corporate Client, Inc. has incurred the following attorneys' fees and expenses in this matter.

Hours:	Partner	4.8 hours	$300/hour	$1,440.00
	Associate	23.6 hours	$210/hour	$4,956.00
	Paralegal	3.2 hours	$90/hour	$288.00
	Totals:	**31.6 hours**		**$6,684.00**
Expenses:	Copy:			$58.25
	Legal research:			$6.32
	Total:			**$64.57**
TOTAL FEES AND EXPENSES:				**$6,748.57**

8. Redacted[1] invoices outlining these fees and expenses are attached hereto collectively as **Exhibit "A"** and incorporated herein by reference for all purposes.
9. The rates charged by my firm in working this file and representing Corporate Client, Inc.'s interests in this matter were reasonable and comparable to other attorneys performing [insert] work in the Anytown legal community.
10. It is my opinion, based on my extensive experience in [*insert*], that the time spent and rates my firm charged in pursuing this matter for Corporate Client, Inc. were fair and reasonable and that the requested attorney's fees and expenses should be approved.

1. Attorney-client communications and sensitive or proprietary work product references have been redacted from the invoices to protect the respective privileges.

Further affiant saith not,

____

SENIOR PARTNER
STATE OF ANYSTATE
COUNTY OF ANYCOUNTY

BEFORE ME, the undersigned authority, personally appeared Senior Partner, who is

______ personally, known to me, or

______ provided proper identification

Type:

and who, upon being first duly sworn according to law, deposes and says that he executed the foregoing Affidavit, and it is true and correct to the best of his knowledge and belief.

IN WITNESS WHEREOF, I have hereunto set my hand and affix the seal of my office in the County and State last aforementioned this _____ day of _____________, ______.

[stamp]

INDEX

ABA Model Rule 1.5, 9
ABA Model Rule 8.4(c), 10
Affidavit to establish fees, 64

Billing in detail, 59–66
Communications, 63
Legal research, 60
Billing system, 93–102
Billable tasks, 75–80
Adding/revising legal arguments, 30
Client review and input, 45
Compiling documents to produce, 39
Court notifications for your own filings, 49
Drafting motions and briefs, 29
Final review and finalization, 46
Legal research, 31
Medical records summaries, 34
Note taking, 51
Preparing separate sections of substantial briefs, 32
Prep time, 49
Receipt of court notifications, 47
Reviewing documents produced in discovery, 36
Review of exhibits, 44
Selection of exhibits, 46
Thinking about a case, 52
Billable time, increasing the amount of, 72–74
Block billing, 23–24

Cases cited
Copeland v. Marshall, 10
Ecos, Inc. v. Brinegar, 41
Francis v. Atlantic Infiniti, Ltd., 80

Grendel's Den, Inc. v. Larkin, 98
Grievson v. Rochester Psychiatric Ctr., 59
Hensley v. Eckerhart, 11, 30
In re Arlan's Dept. Stores, Inc., 12
In re Damon, 12
In re Wash. Pub. Power Supply Sys. Sec. Litig., 10
Kirsch v. Fleet St., Ltd. (quoted in Tatum v. City of N.Y.), 59
Kronfeld v. Transworld Airlines, Inc., 41
LeRoy v. City of Houston, 38
Lindy Bros. Builders, Inc. v. Am. Radiator & Standard Sanitary Corp., 11, 23, 24
Marino v. Denevi, 98
Richardson v. Byrd, 81
U.S.A. v. Boggins, 32
U.S.A. v. Thompson, 32
Williams v. N.Y. City Housing Auth. (quoted in Handschu v. Special Svcs. Div.), 25
Client billing guidelines, 67–70
Client involvement, 26
Client task codes, 70–71

Descriptive titles, 28
Document review, 37

Ethical billing, 9–10

Filing under seal, 63–64
Final review, 40
Formal names, 28

Inner-office meetings, 77–80

Memo to the file, 40
Missing tasks, 55–58

Paralegal time
Case calendars, 88
Draft pleadings and letters, 91
Enclosure letters, 82–83
Materials for a hearing/meeting, 81–82
Medical records, 88
Public records searches, 85–87
Receipt of court pleadings, 87
Scheduling, 84
Physical appearances, 54–55
Placeholders, 94–100
Point-ones, 20–21
Polish language, 94–100

Redundant entries, 30–31

Sample time sheets, 4–6

Task billing, 19
Timekeeping software, 103–105
To/from entries, 27
Travel time, 75–76

ABOUT THE AUTHOR

ANNIE DIKE is a trial and litigation attorney who was admitted to practice in the State of Alabama in 2007, and formerly the N.D.Ala., M.D.Ala., S.D.Ala., and N.D.Fla. Ms. Dike was also admitted to practice law in the State of Florida in 2020. While actively practicing, she focused her practice on medical malpractice, insurance defense, and creditor's rights. She now works remotely (from a sailboat!) and provides litigation support, legal research, motion practice, and appellate brief drafting assistance to a number of attorneys in Florida. Annie graduated from the University of Alabama School of Law *cum laude* in May of 2007. While in law school, she served as Vice President of both the Bench and Bar Legal Honor Society and the Farrah Law Society and was a member of the Alabama Trial Advocacy Competition Team as well as Lead Articles Editor of *The Journal of the Legal Profession*. Ms. Dike has published articles in *The Alabama Lawyer* and *DRI MedLaw Update* and has spoken on numerous legal issues at various conferences nationwide.